WRITING

STEP-BY-STEP

6 Manuscripts in 1 Book, Including: How to Write a Novel, How to Write a Screenplay, Outlining, Story Structure, Plotting and Character Development

Sandy Marsh

Table of Contents

HOW TO WRITE A NOVEL

STEP-BY-STEP

ESSENTIAL ROMANCE NOVEL, MYSTERY NOVEL AND FANTASY NOVEL WRITING TRICKS ANY WRITER CAN LEARN

SANDY MARSH

BOOK 1: HOW TO WRITE A NOVEL

STEP-BY-STEP

Essential Romance Novel, Mystery Novel and Fantasy Novel Writing Tricks Any Writer Can Learn

Sandy Marsh

reparation, damages, or monetary loss due to the information herein, either directly or indirectly.

Respective authors own all copyrights not held by the publisher.

The information herein is offered for informational purposes solely, and is universal as so. The presentation of the information is without contract or any type of guarantee assurance.

The trademarks that are used are without any consent, and the publication of the trademark is without permission or backing by the trademark owner. All trademarks and brands within this book are for clarifying purposes only and are the owned by the owners themselves, not affiliated with this document.

Table of Contents

Introduction

Thank you and congratulations on purchasing *"How to Write a Novel: Step-by-Step | Essential Romance Novel, Mystery Novel and Fantasy Novel Writing Tricks Any Writer Can Learn"*. As well, congratulations on deciding that you want to write a fiction novel!

The tips and tricks you will learn in this book will help walk you through the step-by-step process of writing your very own novel, while also making it extremely easy to stay committed! You will learn everything you need to know about simplifying the process and making it one that you can easily stick to so that you can create the fiction novel of your dreams, literally!

Each chapter in this book is dedicated to one part of the novel writing experience. You will begin by learning all about outlines and work your way through each step right down to finding the perfect reader to test out your new novel. By the time you're done reading this you will be completely finished writing your very own fiction novel.

This book was designed to help make the process easier while also making it an enjoyable experience. Understand that this is not necessarily a "conventional" how-to book as it will seek to both educate and inform while also making the process fun and exciting. Writing a book should never be boring or difficult - if it is, you are going about it all wrong! With the steps in this book, you will learn to bring back the passion in your writing and create the best fiction novel possible, whether this is your first time trying or you've done this before and you just need a boost to get through this particular book!

Please be sure to take your time and have fun with this book as the writing process truly is an experience to be enjoyed. Allow each section to provide you with tips and tricks to help lighten up the experience so that you can increase the entertainment you derive from the writing process so that you are left not only with an incredible novel but also with an experience worth remembering. This book can be used as many times as you require, so be sure to keep it handy for any fiction novels you may set out to write! And lastly, please enjoy!

Chapter 1: The Outline

As you may be aware, having an outline to a book is important. This provides you with an idea of where the story is going and what your "goals" for the book are. Many authors prefer to start with a strong outline that will give them direction and help them stay on track when they are working through the writing process. Having a strong outline that identifies major plot points means that you can continually work your story towards each new plot point in chronological order so that you ultimately end up at your "goal" outcome based on what you had included in your outline.

For many writers, an outline is an absolute must-have. They prefer to have an outline that will help guide them because this keeps them focused and working along a credible storyline that is intended to keep readers engaged. By having this the writer knows how to stay on point and how to structure different parts of the story to keep everything working towards the same goal. For others, having an outline feels too boxy and they feel as though their creative expression is being suffocated by the existence of the outline. If this is you, then you may want to consider scratching the outline altogether. Below we will explore different tips and ideas for each unique individual and how you can create an incredible story regardless of whether or not you choose to use an outline.

If You Love to Guide Your Focus…

If you love to have your focus guided towards a particular goal, such as the one at the end of your outline, then having an outline is a good idea for you. This will help encourage you to stay on track with your writing process and keep each unique element of the story focused towards the outcome. Having the outline helps you avoid yourself from putting unnecessary information in the plot line or otherwise over-explaining things that may not be relevant to the overall story itself.

Outlines are a great tool to help keep writers focused and guided throughout the process. Creating an outline is fairly simple, you think of where you want the characters to "start" and "end" in the story. Then, you decide what major plot points are going to get them from the start to the end. For example, you might have two characters in a romance novel that are going to start as best friends and end as lovers. Along the way, you might choose to include plot points such as them taking on a big project together and it brings them closer, but the competitiveness between them drives them apart. As they work through the competitiveness they discover that their relationship grows even stronger and when they complete the project they are feeling closer than ever before. Later they make excuses to hang out even more, and eventually, they end up falling in love. As you can see from this example, the outline included the main characters, the starting and ending points of the story, and major events that lead the two characters to the "finish line".

Once you have created your basic outline, you want to include even more information in it. This would include settings where each scene takes place, the emotions behind each experience, and anything else that would contribute to you setting the mental image for the scene itself. By identifying as many descriptive factors about each major plot point as possible you make it easier for you to know exactly where you are working towards in each part of the story. Of course, you can always choose to alter these if the writing process brings you towards a different idea or plot point, but having them identified and a rough outline created can help you stay on track and remain focused on what you want to take place within' the story.

If you are someone who tends to need tools such as outlines to help you stay focused and guide you through the process it is a good idea that you complete one before you start writing any part of your novel. Having the outline written and in front of you can help you identify what you like about the story and any issues that you may notice before you actually begin writing. This can help you finalize what your conflict will be an anchor in any specific details that you want to include in your writing so that you go into your novel with a clear plan and an idea of how you are going to achieve what you have set out to accomplish.

If You Love Creative Freedom...

If you are the type of writer who prefers to work alongside creative freedom and who feels suffocated by the idea of having a specific plan to work with there are a few things that you can do in order to exercise your creative freedom while still creating an incredible novel. Just because you don't want to have a specific plan doesn't mean that you cannot create some form of a plan that will help you stay focused and work towards some form of goal throughout your novel.

It is important to understand that even if you prefer having creative freedom, you still need to have some form of outline in place to help you organize your plot and stay focused towards a particular goal. This will help ensure that your book flows in such a way that people will read it and easily work towards the goal with you, rather than attempting to understand why there are so many different pieces of information floating around that seem irrelevant to the book itself.

The first idea you could use is to create a vague outline for your book. This would require you to create an ideal starting point and ending point for your novel, and then fill out the inside of the outline with a few different major plot points that will help guide you from point a to point b. Unlike a complete outline, you will only include enough information to give you a general idea of what you want to include in your book. Then, you can come up with the rest as you are in the process of writing your novel. This can help you with allowing you to have creative expression while also staying focused on the purpose of your novel and working towards it while successfully bringing your reader along with you. Ultimately, it prevents the buildup of irrelevant information or you involving anything that is not necessary to the novel itself.

It will, however, allow you to pick out the details and other smaller factors as you go so that you can allow the story to flow through you naturally, rather than feeling pressured to use extremely specific points in varying areas of your story, potentially taking away from the natural flow that you have created through your creative expression.

Another method you can use is called a hindsight outline. The only two things you need to identify in the beginning of creating this outline is the starting and ending points. You should always have some form of end goal when it comes to writing a novel so that you are clear on what you are writing towards and what you need to be building up to throughout the novel. However, with a hindsight outline, you do not need to include any information beyond these two points. All you have to do is ensure that you are working towards the end goal. As you write major plot points into your story, you can then write them into your outline. This may seem irrelevant, but you will soon understand that writing them down allows you to see where you have come from and where you want to go. It ensures that each part of the plot works together towards the goal and that it makes sense towards the overall story. Doing this prevents you from forgetting about plot points, including ones that may contradict previous ones, and get a general idea of the flow of your story in retrospect, rather than in advance.

Questions to Ask Yourself

The following questions are questions you should ask yourself when you are developing your outline. This will ensure that you have a strong plan for your outline and that no details are missed out on.

1. Where is my protagonist starting?

2. Where are they at in their life in the beginning of the story?

3. Where is my protagonist ending?

4. Where are they at in their life at the end of the story?

5. What major plot points are getting me to (or have gotten me to) the goal?

6. Do these plot points make sense together?

7. Is there anywhere that this outline is weak?

8. What else could I add to my outline to make a rich reading experience?

How you choose to create the outline for your story is unique to you and your writing preferences. Know that you are not required to create a detailed or complete outline before you begin writing your novel. However, having an outline is extremely important as it helps you keep major plot points in chronological order and to ensure that they flow well together. Still, if you prefer to write it out in detail ahead of time, or if you prefer to merely identify your goal and create your outline in hindsight, that is entirely up to you. You should never let creating an outline and identifying specific details of your story hold you back from writing the story in the first place. Knowing that there are options for you to help you stay focused or open up your creative freedom as much as you need to can help ensure that you are not intimidated by the very first step of writing your book. It also helps you feel confident knowing that you can stay focused and still create an incredible book, whether you do it the conventional way or not.

Chapter 2: Your Setting

Developing the setting for your story provides you with the opportunity to have an incredible amount of creative expression. This part of the book is also one of the first times that you will begin to get very descriptive about what is going to happen within' your book. Even if you have a complete outline that is quite detailed, this will be more defined than that.

Your setting is ultimately when and where your story happens. This is something that you need to identify beforehand so that you can keep this information flowing throughout the entire story. For example, you wouldn't want to begin writing a story that was set in the 1800s and then use slang or information that was only relevant to the 2000s or later. Identifying your setting and being very specific and clear on it ensures that your entire book is written with relevance to that setting. The following information will help you identify important tips and tricks that you should pay attention to when it comes to developing your setting for your novel.

If You Only Have One Location

If you are writing a book where the story will never venture away from your primary overall location, then you want to make sure that you are very clear and specific on this location. This is where your entire book is going to be written, so you want to be very descriptive of and clear on this location by knowing exactly what is relevant to it and what is true about it.

You should identify where this location is, what sets it apart from other locations, and why you are using this location. You also want to discover what the local culture is like (specific to your time frame) and any other identifying factors that you may learn about this place. The best way to do it is to research this place as though you were going to be a tourist. Make sure that you do it specific to the time frame, which you will learn more about in a moment. For the location-specific part, however, you want to identify what types of buildings exist in this place, what they were made of, what the roads looked like, what types of wildlife and plant life exists in the area, and anything else that will help you create a graphic image in someone's mind about the location you have chosen.

Once you have identified the location, create a list that involves as many relevant descriptive phrases as you can. You want to generate ideas of how you will describe the place to people throughout the book and creating these ideas beforehand will ensure that you are not at a loss for words or repeating your descriptions throughout the book. Having this list will help you create a dynamic description that truly helps bring the book to life for your readers and prevents them from becoming bored of the same descriptions being used over and over again.

If You Have Many Locations

If you have many locations you want to essentially conduct what you did for one location, only for many. This part of the process may seem fairly straightforward, so we are not going to further explore the process for identifying each unique location. However, there are other things you need to consider when you are using many locations in your book.

First, you want to decide which location is going to be "home" for your characters. This one, in addition to the one where your characters stay in for the longest period of time, should be the ones that you know about the most. You should have plenty of describing factors that help set the scene for what home is like for your characters, as well as for what their new place of residence is like. For example, you might set the scene for home as "The Rocky Mountains: a place where the air is cool and crisp, and the mountainous view is one that cannot be done justice short of seeing it yourself. The community is warm and cozy, especially in the cold winters when snow makes it difficult just to leave your front door." Whereas the new place of residence is described as "The prairies, where the wheat grows for miles and you can see the entire story of the sky as clouds dance across the wide-open view in front of you. The communities are cheerful and bright, and you feel like there is nowhere you can't go, and nothing to stop you from getting where you want to be." You want to describe both the location as previously mentioned and go into detail about the emotion behind each location and why these emotions differ for the protagonist.

Second, you want to identify the mode of travel if any will be used in the book. You also want to become as descriptive as possible when it comes to the mode of transport. Where does the character get on and off of it? What stands out about this mode of transport and how does it contribute to the overall story? Is there anything particular that the reader should know that will help them feel as though they are genuinely walking up to, entering, riding, and exiting the mode of transport that you have chosen? Describing the transport itself in advance will help when it comes to foreshadowing and other story-telling tactics during the writing process. Rather than leaving it up to surprise you can easily blend it into your story so that it flows effortlessly with everything you have already written up until that point, and afterward.

If You Are Making Up the Location

If you are writing a fantasy novel where you are going to be making the location up, it is important that you take the time to actually create a location that makes sense. The location you create needs to be consistent and should be relevant to the story you are telling. There are a few tips when it comes to making up a location that you can consider using to help you create an incredible location for your book.

First, consider basing your location off of somewhere that already exists. If there is somewhere on the globe that resembles what you want your fantasy world to look like, consider first creating a descriptive location setting for that place and then alternating parts of it to fulfill your fantasy world. This will assist you with keeping everything relevant and consistent across your world.

If you are going to be making up the world entirely then you want to take your time. Close your eyes and picture this world in your own mind, first. Then, write as many descriptive factors as you can about the appearance of this location. Ultimately, you want the reader to see exactly what you are seeing in your mind at the time.

You want to make sure that when you are introducing readers to your fantasy world that they feel as though they are mentally stepping into it. They should be able to find enough information in your novel that they can not only step into the world, but they can also interact with it. They should know what type of wildlife - if any - exists in the world. Give them an idea of what the colors are like, how the communities are built, what the buildings themselves look like, and what smells they can find floating around in the air. Give them an idea of what objects are around the setting so that they can mentally picture them and that they truly feel as though they are living in your imaginary world alongside your characters. This will provide you with a strong fantasy setting that will ensure that your book truly is a fantastic read.

If You Only Have One Time Period

When it comes to time periods you need to be very specific and careful. You want to choose one that would make sense to and be relevant to the story you are telling. You also want to ensure that you do enough research about it that you tell the story as though it truly is set in that time frame. A painful mistake that would truly detract from the value of your novel would be one where you choose a certain time frame and then include information that is completely irrelevant to that time frame. For example, if you chose to set your romance novel in the late 1900s but included technology such as cell phones or computers, it would not make sense to the story and would take away from the reading experience.

When you are setting the time frame you want to ensure that you do plenty of research about it. You also want to research your chosen location with relevance to the time frame. What did it look like during that time frame? What was the culture like? What were the people like? How did they treat each other? What was the common slang for that era? You want to be very specific on what it truly would have been like during that time frame so that you can walk your reader through it. Give them the opportunity to feel as though they have stepped into a time portal and they are being transported into that era, whether it be in the present or in the past.

If You Have Many Time Periods

When you are writing a story that has many time periods the tactics you use to develop the setting is similar to if you are writing a story that has many locations. Essentially, you want to ensure that you are effectively researching each time period so that you can provide relevant and factual information based on each time period. You really need to stay focused on the details you are providing so that your reader can easily be walked back and forth with you without finding irrelevant or false pieces of information anywhere within' the text. The more focused and factual you are, the better. When it comes to developing many time periods in a story, there is not much more required than you repeating the research processes several times over for each time period you will write about. Something you may want to add, however, is the mode of transportation being used to transport across time periods. Be sure that you create a piece of machinery and provide enough details about it that you can explain how it works and create a graphic image of it in the minds of your readers.

If You Are Making up the Time Period

If you are making up a time period in your novel, then you need to be extremely descriptive about this time period. You should identify what the time period is, and why it does not already exist. For example, maybe you are generating your own fantasy setting on an alternate planet and Earth has yet to exist therefore the time is not yet in history. Or, perhaps you are writing one in the future and the time has not happened yet, so you are creating it yourself. You need to be able to thoroughly understand *why* you are creating this new time period so that your readers understand as well.

In addition to knowing why, you also need to make up all of the important details about the time period. What is the culture like in this time period? What form of government or authority exists? What do people speak like? Are there any slang words used that your readers may not already know? What do these slang words mean? How do people treat each other? What parts of the community are different from anything we experience in our own world? What else sets this time period apart from what you are presently living or what we already know about? You want to make sure that you go into detail beforehand about creating this time period so that when it comes to the writing process you already know. Doing this will ensure that you stay consistent with your novel and that nothing is added that is then forgotten about and later contradicted. When you are making something up entirely it is important that you put the effort in towards making it truly believable for your readers. This will ensure that they are able to follow the story and that it flows well without having any contradictions, confusing pieces of information, or other additions that otherwise take away from the quality of the story itself.

Combining the Two

The setting of your story is a combination of the time period and the location. When you have completely researched or created each the location and the time period, you must then combine the two. This part of the process is simple, but it is important. You want to make sure that you identify anywhere in the combination where information might contradict itself or take away from the reading experience. For example, if you are writing a book set in the present about an Amish colony that still operates without running water or electricity, you need to identify these factors and explain the discrepancy. Making sure that your time and location mesh together seamlessly and that anything contradictory is explained will ensure that you have a strong setting for your story. This means that you will be able to easily and effortlessly guide your readers through the book without any part of it leading to them wondering what is truly going on with your story.

Questions to Ask Yourself

The following questions are questions you should ask yourself when you are developing your setting. This will ensure that you have a strong plan for your setting and that no details are missed out on.

1. What location(s) will my story take place in?

2. What is unique to this location?

3. How could I describe this location in five sentences or less?

4. When I read that description, can I truly see the location in my mind?

5. Are there any further descriptions I could use to strengthen the visual of my location?

6. What time period(s) will my story take place in?

7. What is unique to this time period?

8. How could I describe this location in five sentences or less?

9. When I read that description, can I truly feel and sense the time period in my mind?

10. Are there any further descriptions I could add to enrich the time period in my story?

11. Do my time period and location make sense together?

12. What describing factors can I use to explain any
    discrepancies between my location and time period,
    if there are any?

Chapter 3: The Point of View

The next part of writing your story requires you to consider which point of view you want to write from. As an author, you have the opportunity to decide exactly how the reader is going to learn about different elements of your story, as well as how those elements will feel to them. You can do this directly through the use of point of view and which you choose to write your story in.

There are a few different points of view that you can write from when it comes to storytelling. Each one has a unique element that allows you to elaborate on and recall experiences within' the story in a certain way. Some will limit you to only telling it from one perspective whereas others allow you to elaborate with multiple perspectives, or even to provide "outsiders" insight into different experiences. How you choose your point of view will also depend on a few things. Before you choose one, however, let's explore each unique point of view and the advantages and disadvantages it provides you with as a storyteller.

First Person

First person point of view is one of the most popular choices when it comes to writing novels. This is the point of view where the writer refers to the narrator as "I", "we", "me", "mine", "my", and "us". This is similar to if you were telling a story from your own past to someone who was standing in front of you. When you are telling a story from the first-person point of view you must pick which protagonist is going to be the storyteller in your book. Typically, it is the heroic character or the one that is involved in the majority of the scenes that will be chosen as the first-person narrator. However, you can choose virtually anyone you want, dependent upon who is going to be the best angle for you to speak from.

When you write in the first person, you provide a very natural flow to your story. Your reader will feel as though you are telling them *your* story, and if you can effectively captivate them then it will actually begin to feel like your reader is the narrator. Using "I" sentiments and first-person narrative allows your reader to fully immerse themselves in the novel and get a true, deep insight into how the narrator was feeling during each scene. You also only have to pay attention to and fully develop the mind of one character: the narrators. This is the one that you will need to have the most insight to. The rest will be based on how the narrator perceives them, which means that you don't have to go quite as deep or know every minute detail of each person. However, this can also lead to some disadvantages. For example, you are limited to only reflecting on and elaborating the story based on what the narrator would feel. You cannot explore anyone else's feelings unless you use tactics such as conversation to help the narrative character explore the feelings and thoughts of another. While this is an effective tactic, you aren't going to be able to use it in every single scene or the story will sound strange and unnatural. Furthermore, the narrative character must always be involved in or at the center of every event that takes place in the book. Otherwise, large portions are going to be missed or you are going to bounce between different points of view which is not effective.

Some ways that people have managed to use the first-person narrative while still maintaining the insights on several characters at once is by developing books whereby each chapter or section is narrated by a different character. This provides the reader with the opportunity to see into several different characters and their experiences, but it can also jolt the flow of your story and result in your readers struggling to really connect with each character the way they could if you maintained a single first-person narrative.

Second Person

Second person is an undesirable choice when it comes to writing fiction, but some people choose to use it when they are writing short stories. This is an interesting point of view to write from, but it rarely creates the ability for an author to produce an entire novel without the novel sounding strange and lacking natural flow. Second person is the "you" narrative, whereby you refer to the person reading or the narrator as "you". For example, "you were standing on a street corner when suddenly someone bumped into you." The entire book would be written in this point of view which, as you might be able to tell, is not ideal. While some books have been written this way, most publishers advise against it and will even refuse to publish books that have been written in this narrative.

The only advantage to writing in the second person narrative is that your book will be unique and eccentric. Based on the nature of this narrative you gain the ability to speak directly to the reader which can be an interesting technique, but it also does not offer you a strong advantage in storytelling. For the most part, anything written in the second person narrative that is longer than a few hundred words feels uncomfortable and sounds "off" to the reader. They will likely grow tired of the eccentric feel and simply begin feeling as though the writing is uncomfortable and strange. Furthermore, it says that you are unprofessional and are inexperienced when it comes to novels. Unless you are a highly experienced writer who has already developed a name for themselves, it is typically best that you avoid this point of view.

Third Person

Third person is the point of view whereby someone completely outside of the story is telling it. For example, using identifiers such as "he" or "she" instead of "I" or "you". This point of view is another popular one when it comes to writing fiction novels because it provides the author with the ability to provide insight into many different elements of each character. It also provides the author with a greater ability to influence the reader's emotions towards various characters without that influence being limited to what would be true and natural for any given character within' the book. For example, perhaps the protagonist hates the antagonist for something he's done wrong. In the first person, you would be required to establish feelings of hatred towards the antagonist. In the third person, however, you can further explain the situation and provide the reader with insight as to how it was a mistake and the protagonist was carrying a grudge over something that was a misunderstanding, for example. It provides you with a stronger power to shape and influence the story in a highly unique way.

When it comes to writing in the third party there are two different types you can write in: third person limited omniscience, or third person unlimited omniscience. Since each one is so unique, we are going to explore them in two different subsections below.

Before we dive in, however, please note that in the following subsections we will discuss a tool many authors use whereby they speak in the third person from a different character's point of view in each scene or chapter. This helps naturally break up the story without confusing the reader along the way. This should not be confused with the technique whereby authors write one chapter per character from the first-person point of view. Although the techniques are virtually the same, they do involve writing from a different point of view in each style.

Third Person Limited Omniscience

Third person limited omniscience means that the author has the power to enter the mind of only a few characters within' the novel. Usually, during this type of experience, the author would write from the point of view of one character per chapter or per scene to avoid confusion. When it comes to this viewpoint, the author would still write with the "he" or "she" descriptors, but would primarily focus on one character per scene or chapter.

This point of view provides the author with the opportunity to enrich the experience by providing viewpoints from many different characters, thereby giving the reader a greater amount of detail and depth into each scene and experience within' the book. It also provides the author the opportunity to write from a broader scope where they are not required to limit their story to a single person's experiences. Instead, you can elaborate on experiences that may take place without one or more of the character's present. The biggest disadvantage of this is that for the author it requires you to take more time to make each part of the book flow naturally, as well as to provide distinctive voices for each character so as not to confuse yourself or your reader. Furthermore, if you switch too often you will break up the flow of your story and create an unnatural and uncomfortable. It is important that you take your time and truly dedicate if you are going to use this practice, also. Many authors find that they write in this point of view for a few chapters and then they wind up writing from the first-person narrative for the remainder of the book. This laziness can result in your first chapters, or last chapters needing to be repaired so that the entire book is written in the same narrative and flows smoothly.

Third Person Unlimited Omniscience

Third person, unlimited omniscience is virtually the same as limited omniscience, except that the author is not restricted to only sharing the experience from a few character's points of view. Instead, they can shift into the mind of any character within' the story and provide their viewpoint on the events that are taking place.

While this may provide the author with the opportunity to elaborate and provide great detail and depth to the story, it can also result in them getting far too carried away if they are not careful. Writing from too many different points of view can diffuse the entire story and result in the author washing out any storyline that may have taken place. It is similar to the mistake of oversharing or otherwise providing far too much information, well beyond what the reader needs to know. Although it may give them a strong understanding of each scene, it can also cause for it to take far too long to "get to the point already". It is generally advised against the idea of you writing in third person unlimited omniscience unless you are using the technique strategically to avoid damaging your storyline.

How to Choose

There is one incredibly each tactic to use when it comes to deciding which point of view you want to use when it comes to sharing your story. Consider taking one small scene from the book and then writing that scene in three different narratives: first person, third person limited omniscience, and third person unlimited omniscience. Only write a few short paragraphs in each point of view so that it doesn't take too long, but be sure that you write them well. Then, read each one. This will give you an idea as to how each point of view would shape the reader's experience and what "feel" it gives to your story. It also provides you with some practice as to how each point of view feels as the author and if it gives you the ability to express yourself in the way that you want to be expressed.

Questions to Ask Yourself

The following questions are questions you should ask yourself when you are choosing your point of view. This will ensure that you have a strong plan for your point of view and that no details are missed out on.

1. Who do I want to tell my story?

2. What feeling do I want my readers to have?

3. Which point of view is going to be reasonable for me to write an entire novel in?

4. Will this give me the opportunity to express my
    story the way I want to?

5. Is there any way that this might limit my story or
    otherwise hinder the reader's experience?

Chapter 4: Characters

Naturally, your story needs characters. After all, what story are you telling if there is no one taking part in the story itself? Creating a strong story requires for you to have strong, well-developed characters involved. If you are looking for greater insight as to how you can develop well-rounded characters I encourage you to read book 6 from this series: "*Character Development*: Step-by-Step." Because I provide you with such great detail on how to develop your characters in that novel, I will not go into elaborate detail on character development in this chapter. Instead, we are going to identify other important information about your characters, such as who needs to be involved in the story and how they contribute. Knowing this basic information is powerful in regard to the actual writing process. This will help you when it comes to outlining and creating a plan for the direction of your story. When it comes to the actual writing process, however, you will want to make sure that you have fully developed characters so that they are realistic and can add to your story in a powerful way. In the meantime, let's explore other important aspects of characters in your story.

The Value of Your Characters

Characters are a powerful element of your story because they truly drive the story forward. Without characters, the story simply cannot move forward because there would be nothing to talk about. Your characters help you not only convey the story but also express it in certain ways. Depending on what point of view you have chosen, your characters can be used in unique ways to manipulate the reader's thoughts and feelings about other characters, as well as about the storyline and events that take place within' the story.

Think of professional dancers. Music is put on as the foundation for the story and it can be related to the setting. The words that coincide with the music, or the song lyrics, are responsible for providing you with insight into what the song is about. Once the dancers begin dancing, however, they can manipulate how you feel about the song, what emotions are provoked within' you, and how you take in the experience as a whole. Without the dancers, it would simply be a song with lyrics. With the dancers, it is a story with a soul.

The same goes with writing books. The setting is the foundation for your story, and the narrator is the one who tells the story. Your characters, however, provide the heart and soul of your story. They are the ones that you can use to help manipulate the readers' thoughts and provoke different emotions in them so that they experience the book in the way that you want them to. While each unique reader may have a slightly different experience, the overall interpretation of the book will remain fairly similar if you use your tools or characters, properly.

Choosing Your Protagonist

Because of how important characters are, it is vital that you choose a good character to be your protagonist. Your protagonist needs to be a strong character who can lead the story in a powerful way. When you are putting together the outline and idea for your story, consider which specific character would be best at bringing readers through the story in an effective manner that would allow you to create the experience you want to create. Which of your characters will be involved in the most experiences? Which ones will have the best emotional attachment to the storyline so that they can move your readers for you? If you are writing from a first-person narrative, you need to choose a single character that is going to be able to effectively move everyone through the entire novel. For example, it may be the wife, best friend, teacher, and book club host. Because this particular character is involved in so many different elements of the community she may be the best individual and voice to help you tell the story with a great level of depth and dynamic so that the reader truly has an incredible experience. If you are writing in the third party, however, make sure that you choose powerful characters that you will write from. These would-be ones that all connect in one way or another and that have stories that will link together. This ensures that each character makes sense to the narrative. If you are writing in third-party unlimited omniscience, make sure that when you move to the narrative of someone who may be new or unique to a specific part of the story that this move makes sense and it is clear to the reader as to why you are doing this. This will ensure that you are drawing the reader through a clear and logical storyline that makes sense.

How Many Characters Do You Really Need?

The number of characters you choose to have in your story is really unique to the story you are trying to tell. If you are telling a romance novel, for example, you may only have two primary characters and a handful of other characters that contribute to the story. For example, some best friends, family members, the cashier at the drug store they always stop at, or the receptionist at the hotel where they celebrate their honeymoon. When you are planning your story, you need to consider how many characters are actually going to be required in order for you to tell the story. As you carry on you may discover that you need to add more characters along the way, so it is not mandatory for you to identify every single character you are going to write about immediately. However, you should have a good idea of who your primary and secondary characters are going to be. Remember, your primary characters are the ones that show up in nearly all scenes and your secondary ones are characters that are recurring in a major way.

What Your Characters Say About Your Book

The characters you choose are going to say a lot about the book you are writing and the story you are telling. These characters have the power to shape the reader's perception of the book, as well as gain an even deeper insight as to what the setting is like and the feelings they should be deriving from the general information you are providing. For example, if you are writing a book from the late 1990's about a town in the southern states, you could write about a wealthy family or a poor family. This would shape your character's point of view on the entire setting and emotions associated with the book, as well as how they perceive your characters. It also helps round out your story. The characters you choose, how you design them, and how you portray them will all contribute to the story you tell. In the previous example, one story might provide the reader with a country glamorous feeling where they ride horses and own a large farm with stable hands, whereas the other might provide your family with a poorer country feel where they *are* the stable hands and they live in a shack built on the corner of the property. Who you choose for your characters will provide greater depth for your story and ultimately be the final factor that provides your reader with the clear picture of what they see, think, and feel as they read the story you have written for them.

Questions to Ask Yourself

The following questions are questions you should ask yourself when you are developing the basic outline for your characters. This will ensure that you have a strong plan for your character development and that no details are missed out on. Remember to check out book 6 where we go deeper into the creation and development of characters so that you have a strong selection of characters to help move your story forward.

1. What story am I telling and who is the focus of the story?

2. What point of view am I writing in and whose point of view do I want to write from?

3. What recurring characters are an important element of this story?

4. Are there any additional characters that will be involved in key plot points?

5. How do these specific characters help move the story?

Chapter 5: Conflict

Every good novel comes with a fair amount of conflict involved. If there was no conflict, then there would be nothing that really keeps the reader engaged. Everyone loves a great happy-ending story, but most like to see the work that goes into creating that happy ending. This is somewhat like providing a realistic snippet of your character's lives to your readers. No one's real life is easy all of the time, so writing an entire novel where all of your characters never experience any true conflict is not only unrealistic but also boring. It takes away from the entire reading experience by never giving any depth or diversity to your story.

Creating conflict in your novel should be an ongoing process. It is not simply about having one major conflict and everything being sunshine and rainbows up until and after that point. Instead, it is about leading up to the conflict, and about coming down from it as well. You want to have one primary conflict that drives the story, but you should include many other conflicts along the way as well. These smaller conflicts add more depth and reality to your story, but they also help you lead your reader through many triumphs and victories with the characters. Each time your character overcomes something your reader will feel as though they overcame it together and it will bond the reader to your character even more. Furthermore, it stops you from writing an unrealistic story that goes from bad to much worse and then suddenly great again. It provides you with a natural and lifelike flow that allows your reader to feel as though they are genuinely connecting with an individual and not a character that you have made up for the purpose of writing a novel.

Types of Conflict

There are a couple of different types of conflict that exist in every novel. The first one is considered a primary conflict. This is the primary purpose of why you are telling the story, and it is what you will lead up to and wind down from throughout the process of writing the novel. This is the "big one" that will keep your readers engaged and have them feeling like they *need* to know what happens after that particular conflict takes place.

The next type is secondary conflict. This is the type of conflict that takes place leading up to and after the primary conflict. These are smaller conflicts that exist in addition to the primary conflict. For example, maybe in an action-based novel the kidnapper is about to drive a car off of a bridge, so the protagonist has to go save the person who has been kidnapped, but they can't do that until they can get a car because the kidnapper has their car. Here, the kidnapper driving off the bridge would be the primary conflict and the lack of a car would be the secondary conflict. In the grand scheme of the entire story, however, both would be secondary to the greater problem which is that someone has been kidnapped. When you build on the conflict in this way it diversifies everything and adds a more realistic and compelling story base that drives readers forward. Now, they want to know where the protagonist gets the car from if they reach the kidnapper on time, and how they save the person who has been kidnapped. As you can see, it would keep them engaged.

The third type of conflict is an alternate conflict. In a story where third person point of view is used, the author may choose to have two or three primary conflicts going on. For example, for the parents getting divorced might be the primary conflict, for one kid her social life falling apart might be the primary conflict, and for the second kid choosing which parent to live with might be the primary conflict. This story would run with each of these conflicts equally as important as the other, and each one drives part of the story forward until it all reaches an ending whereby everyone is satisfied and happy with the outcome.

When the Conflict Should Occur

Choosing when the conflict should occur in your book is important. There are many different points at which you might desire to put the primary conflict into your plotline. However, it is imperative that you give your reader a reason to care by infusing some form of conflict into the first ten pages.

Some authors choose to start out within' the first ten pages by introducing the primary conflict and then providing the remainder of the wind-down story from there. For example, elaborating further on the plotline where someone is kidnapped, you may write that said person was kidnapped on the first page, or within' the first ten pages. The rest of the book would then be a series of secondary conflicts that result from the primary conflict, until the end where the person is rescued.

Other authors do not want to reveal the primary conflict right away and choose to save it for later. Some prefer to put it somewhere in the middle of the book and provide a fairly even amount of writing leading up to the conflict and winding down from it, whereas others like to put it towards the end of the story and use the winding down process as the opportunity to introduce the "happily ever after" experience.

Where you prefer to put the conflict in your own story heavily depends on how quickly you want your readers to move through the conflict, as well as how you want the conflict to leverage the story overall. If you want it to be the primary focus of the story, you may want to introduce it sooner or at least use secondary conflicts to suggest it starting right away. However, if you want the happily-ever-after story to be the primary focus of the story then you may want to use more casual secondary conflicts to keep the reader engaged while building them up to the conflict and then using the resolution as your final happily-ever-after scene.

Regardless of how you choose to infuse the story with your conflict, one thing remains consistent: you need to give the reader a reason to continue reading your book. Within' the first ten pages your reader needs to understand why they should fall in love with the book through developing relationships with the characters, understanding the importance of the conflicts and how they affect the characters, and what they can expect to feel when reading the book. All of this can be done by how you introduce the conflict, and when.

Questions to Ask Yourself

The following questions are questions you should ask yourself when you are developing your conflict. These questions will ensure that you are clear on what your conflict is and how it affects the story you are telling.

1. What is the primary conflict taking place in my novel?

2. How many primary conflicts do I want involved in my novel? (Note: if you are telling a story from the first person, choose one or two at most.)

3. What type of secondary conflicts can I use to build up to the primary conflict?

4. What secondary conflicts would work well to help me wind down from the conflict?

5. How do I want the conflict to drive my novel forward?

6. When do I want to introduce the conflict and how will that affect the reading experience?

7. Does the conflict make sense to the novel?

8. Does the conflict provide enough reason for the reader to truly care?

9. If I am not introducing my primary conflict right away, what conflict can I use to compel my reader to continue reading?

Chapter 6: Additional Tips

In addition to the basics of writing your novel, there are many additional tips that you can use when it comes to generating a high-quality fiction-based novel that will not only impress yourself but your audience as well. Using these tips when you are writing your story will help you increase the joy you get from the process while also increasing the value of your work. These tips are selected from a series of professional writers and have helped them in the process of generating their own fiction novels. Remember, however, not everyone is the same and therefore you may not require all of these tips when it comes to writing your own novel. Take what feels right for you and your unique story and leave the rest!

As mentioned in the introduction of this book, the tips and information provided within' this book is unique and issued to help you not only create higher quality materials but also enjoy the process. Writing your novel should be an experience that you gain joy from, not one that stresses you out or makes you feel incompetent. If you are struggling, you are not doing it right. The following tips can help take you out of the struggling mode and put you back in the mood to enjoy the experience. When the process is light and enjoyable you will likely find that you produce much better work, so be sure to slow down and readdress your approach if you are struggling to produce the results you desire.

Finally, because of the fact that some of these tips may not apply to the unique book you are writing, you will likely want to keep this information handy for any additional projects you may desire to accomplish. Some of these tips may be more relevant to certain types of books than they are to others, therefore you are likely to find value in new and unique ways each time you return to this book.

Think Outside of the Box

When it comes to writing stories, there are many plotlines that exist that are simply rewritten with different angles and different characters. The setting may be different and some of the events that take place may alter, but ultimately the entire story works out to be similar to several other books within' the same genre. Although the saying "don't try to reinvent the wheel" may ring true in many cases, it is not always the best approach to take when you are attempting to write a new and interesting book that will engage your readers in a powerful way.

Instead of trying to recreate a tired plotline, try thinking outside of the box entirely. Consider the genre you are writing for, such as romance, mystery, or fantasy, and spend some time thinking about parts of the story that are never typically told within' traditional novels from that genre. As you discover new parts of the story that you can emphasize on, make sure that you are truly criticizing them to ensure that there is a good reason as to why this part of the story hasn't been told before. Sometimes a certain element may be rejected or ignored because there simply isn't enough to talk about, other times it may be because that isn't the traditional approach, therefore, most people don't consider it when they are writing a novel in that genre.

Looking at things from a different perspective and discovering new ways to share a story provides your book with a unique twist that allows you to engage your readers not only through incredible work but also through the element of surprise. For example, most romance novels lead up to the part where the lovers fall in love, but what if your novel was more focused on the wind-down? What if the marriage happened within' the first ten pages and from there it was the wind-down and told the next part of the romance story that most novels don't focus on? Paying attention to unique elements of the story gives you the opportunity to still write in your chosen genre while also having the chance to put a unique spin on things and create a story that people weren't expecting.

Ditch Expectations

When it comes to the writing world you will likely stumble on expectations from many different people. Publishers, readers, yourself, other authors, everyone has an expectation of what a book "should" be like. While it is important to consider these elements, especially since some of them can make or break the success of your book, it is also important to ditch the pressure that comes along with them.

Most writers can agree that feeling too much pressure can result in writer's block and it can also drown the enjoyment you gain from writing the book. It can make it feel too much like work and less like an experience to be enjoyed by both you and the readers. Instead of putting that much pressure on yourself, ditch expectations and write for the trashcan. You will likely be surprised at the quality of work you produce when you aren't considering all of the technical aspects of your book.

Set Deadlines

Having deadlines set in place can help you keep motivated, and it can also help you plan for other parts of the book writing process. For example, this can help you decide when you need to begin approaching publishers when work needs to be handed in, when marketing efforts should commence, and more. Having deadlines in place keeps everything moving forward and prevents you from avoiding or neglecting your book altogether.

When you are setting deadlines, however, be generous with yourself. Do not set a deadline that is fixed on a date that requires you to work an obscene amount each day from where you are now until the deadline arrives. Doing this will bring back the pressure and take away the joy of the writing experience. Instead of writing and allowing the story to flow through you, you will be writing under the pressure of knowing that if you don't get a certain amount of words out *right now* that you will officially be late for your deadline and everything will be hindered by your lack of writing speed. Instead, choose a generous deadline that gives you plenty of time to take breaks, step aside and get a breather, and come back to your work to finish it. Be kind to yourself and account for breaks. Most writers do not write an entire book in one straight shot. Instead, they write for several days, or even weeks, and then take breaks off in between to allow for more inspiration to come to them before they carry on. Give yourself the opportunity to have these breaks so that you can take them without feeling pressure.

Get a Good "Test" Reader

When your book is complete, you need to have a good test reader who can read through it for you. This is someone who is not necessarily looking for grammatical errors or otherwise editing your book. Rather, they are simply reading to see if it is engaging and if it will actually appeal to your audience. Naturally, this person should identify with your target audience or their opinion may not count for much.

It is important that you do not hand your book to everyone you know and get as many people as possible. Instead, pick one or *maybe* two test readers who identify with your target audience and allow them to read the book. This way you can get honest opinions without feeling overwhelmed by a number of responses you get. It also helps open your purchasing audience because your friends and family will likely be some of your earliest buyers once your title is launched.

Avoid Perfectionism

Many writers put a pressure on themselves to create the perfect piece of work. They may think of an artist they already know or a series of books they have read that they perceive as perfect and they want their books to be the same quality. Understand that this is not valuable to the writing process and it can actually hold you back from producing high-quality work.

Perfectionism can be intimidating, and it can have you overly critical of the work you are producing. Most of the best books that exist on shelves today were not subjected to perfectionism. Instead, the author focused on telling a great story, not a perfect one. Readers are not expecting a perfect book, they are expecting one that takes them through the story in such a way that is engaging and makes them genuinely feel as though they are present and can relate to what they are reading. Perfectionists need not worry.

Write What You Don't Know

There is a long-standing piece of advice that tells writers to "write what they know", but this isn't always the best way to go. Unless you are deeply passionate about your topic and can infuse it with all of the emotions related to that passion, consider writing what you *don't* know.

Think about a topic that interests you and things you would have to learn based on that new interest. Then, spend time researching it for the purpose of writing the book. For example, if your protagonist is a karate star, consider going to a few karate lessons to get a first-hand idea of what it is like so that you can write from within' the experience. Writing in this way gives you a better opportunity to convey the excitement that you are feeling through your story, thus translating it into the reader's experience.

When we write about what we know, we often don't have the same level of excitement or passion as we would if we were brand new to the knowledge because we have a "been there, done that" feeling towards the topic. Even when we are passionate about it, it can be hard to convey that new childlike wonder through the story. When you are brand new, however, it is brand new to you *and* the reader, and it can enhance the quality of your story through all of the exciting emotions you infuse it with.

Manipulate Your Reader's Emotions

Readers are most often attracted to books that draw out a variety of emotions in them. You want to use your characters and the storyline to manipulate your reader's emotions so that they are emotionally drawn to and attached to the book as you are reading. Many readers agree that the best books are the ones that leave you with a "lost" feeling when you put them down. This is because the reader has developed an emotional attachment to the book, likely based on the writer's technique.

You can manipulate your reader's emotions through a variety of different plot points, experiences, and descriptive phrases. You want to start by helping them become emotionally connected to one or more of the characters, then subject these characters to various experiences that draw out certain emotions in the characters. As a result, it will draw out emotions in your readers as well.

When your reader is emotionally connected to the book, they are far more engaged and much more likely to read it all the way through. Furthermore, they are much more likely to genuinely enjoy the book. Make sure that you play with several different emotions so that the book is not excessively sad, angry, funny, or otherwise. Even if you want to emphasize on one emotion more than the rest, be sure to add a healthy mixture of other emotions so that the book does not become predictable or boring.

Conclusion

Thank you for reading *"How to Write a Novel: Step by Step | Essential Romance Novel, Mystery Novel and Fantasy Novel Writing Tricks Any Writer Can Learn"*!

I hope that this book was able to provide you with many tips and tricks to assist you in the process of writing your very own fiction novel. Whether you are writing a romance novel, a mystery novel, or a fantasy novel, I hope that you were able to learn many valuable methods to increase the enjoyment of the experience and increase the quality of your work overall. This book was designed to help you master the writing process, and I hope that you were able to learn plenty of new and diverse information in order to help you do so.

The next step is to start writing! If you haven't already, begin with your outline and move forward from there. As you are working on your book, be sure to check back with this guidebook regularly to see if there are any tips or tricks related to the part of the process you are presently in. This book was written to be a writing resource that you can check back to as often as you need, so don't hesitate to keep it handy during the entire writing process. You never know what part of the book might become valuable to you during each unique part of the process!

Thank you, and enjoy!

HOW TO WRITE A SCREENPLAY

STEP-BY-STEP

ESSENTIAL SCREENPLAY FORMAT, SCRIPTWRITER AND MODERN SCREENPLAY WRITING TRICKS ANY WRITER CAN LEARN

SANDY MARSH

BOOK 2: HOW TO WRITE A SCREENPLAY

STEP-BY-STEP

Essential Screenplay Format, Scriptwriter and Modern Screenplay Writing Tricks Any Writer Can Learn

Sandy Marsh

reparation, damages, or monetary loss due to the information herein, either directly or indirectly.

Respective authors own all copyrights not held by the publisher.

The information herein is offered for informational purposes solely and is universal as so. The presentation of the information is without a contract or any type of guarantee assurance.

The trademarks that are used are without any consent, and the publication of the trademark is without permission or backing by the trademark owner. All trademarks and brands within this book are for clarifying purposes only and are the owned by the owners themselves, not affiliated with this document.

Table of Contents

Introduction

I want to thank you and congratulate you for purchasing the book *"How to Write a Screenplay: Step-by-Step | Essential Screenplay Format, Scriptwriter and Modern Screenplay Writing Tricks Any Writer Can Learn"*.

In this book, you will find all of the information you need to begin writing a screenplay, the details on the specifics of the most common types of screenplays, tips on creating believable characters in your screenplays, how to create a first draft and get to work on editing and tips that have worked for the experts.

You will need the information in this book if you want to create a successful script that will catch the eye of producers to get it to the big screen.

To not develop your ability to write a properly formatted screenplay would be Hollywood murder to your career. Style is everything, and this book covers that.

It's time for you to create an amazing screenplay.

Chapter 1: What is a Screenplay?

A screenplay (also known as a script) is a written output made for a television show, a movie, a video, or a game. When it is written for television, it is also called as teleplay.

Screenplay consists of action and dialogue. Action is where a character is noted to do an action, and a dialogue is where the character is speaking. These two components make up around ninety percent of a screenplay.

What sets a screenplay apart from a stageplay are the use of sluglines. This designates where the scene takes place, and what time of day it is, along with the weather that is occurring at the time. These descriptions are important so that the director can make sure that the scenes are set up properly.

Physical format

Screenplays are printed very specifically. They are also all put together specifically as well. This makes it easier for a producer to get through a bunch at one time. They are generally bound with a cardboard cover and a back page to protect the script when it is handled. Oftentimes, the first copy of the script is the only copy. While it is backed up, it takes a lot of paper to print a script most times, so it is important to save where you can.

In America, the script is usually printed single-spaced on letter size paper. It is printed using 12 point courier font. When it is bound, it is bound using a three-hole punch and held together with two brads. One at the top and one at the bottom. This makes it easier to flip through the script quickly.

Reading copies, those which are distributed, are often printed double-sided to reduce paper waste. This is because there are often more copies that will need to be printed later on, and scripts already take so much paper to print anyway, that finding ways to cut down is a must.

Scripts can often be delivered electronically, but many companies require that a certain amount of copies be handed to the company, or at least mailed if travel is not possible.

Screenplay formats

Screenplays come with a certain set of standards that must be met. These standards are ones that help keep everything uniform and allow for easy reading. They form a sort of blueprint for movies and other screenplays. This also allows a company to distinguish those who take things seriously, from those who have a more laissez-faire attitude. There are software packages out there that can help assist with the formatting of screenplays. This makes it easier to ensure that you will have a professional looking piece to show prospective producers. SmartKey, the first screenwriting software, sent codes to existing word processors. However, the ones today have their own macro entities.

Feature film

If you intend to get a motion picture on the big screen, there are a lot of stipulations for how you have to write your screenplay. The headings, formatting, and spacing all have to meet a specific set of guidelines. While the guidelines may vary from country to country, they are all pretty similar in the fact that they have to be uniform. This is because the rate of transfer from page to screen remains around one minute. This gives a rough estimate of how long the piece will run when taken to the big screen. However, some things often get cut, so it is a very rough estimate.

Nevertheless, if you ever want anybody to not only read what you have written, but to truly take it seriously, you will need to stick to the rules in order to ensure that they have as few obstacles between them and getting to the heart of your story. In general, you can think of the concept of screenplay formatting as mainly an aesthetic choice to ensure that every page of your screenplay is as clear and legible as possible. Each script you turn in should always be written in 12-point, Courier font. This goes for movies or television.

The Slug: Luckily, the Hollywood script format is simple once you learn the basics. Every screenplay is divided into different scenes, each of which represents a different location that the story is viewed from. When a new location is introduced in a screenplay, it needs to be described in a specific way so that the person reading it can automatically picture three key pieces of information. They will need to know whether the scene is taking place inside or outside, the time of day it is and the actual location. Together, these three things form what is known as the slug.

Each scene introduction is going to be written so that it appears on a single line, which will include the location details as well as relevant information about the time of day. The majority of slugs will start with either EXT. or INT., meaning exterior or interior respectively. In general, a slug with start with EXT. or INT. and end with either NIGHT OR DAY unless the specific time of day is crucial to the scene. The only time this will not be the case is during parts of the script where the action is repeatedly cutting between two places or is moving through a number of locations, following a character who starts out from a location that has already been defined. For example: EXT. CAVE – DAY

If you have already introduced the cave in the previous example, then you could simplify by writing BACK TO CAVE.

If a character is moving throughout multiple locations inside a predefined location, such as a house, you can write the intervening slugs as KITCHEN or BEDROOM to maintain the flow of the story while still providing the reader with the details they need.

While not required, the slug often also includes the indicator SUPER which is followed by identifying information and indicates what would be superimposed on the screen for example SUPER: 10 years earlier.

If you are writing a conversation between two individuals who are not speaking to one another directly, you can use the indicator INTERCUT BETWEEN after both of the settings have been determined with a standard slug.

The shot: While the shot will also appear in capital letters with a similar type of formatting, it serves a different function when compared to a slug and shot not be confused with it.

As an example: ANGLE ON JACK, C.U. ON GUN. When writing your screenplay, you will use this technique to draw specific attention to an element of the action. It is typically followed by its own description, almost written as an aside, that is always ended with the indicator BACK TO SCENE before the action from the main scene resumes.

Action elements: An action element is going to come directly after the slug and is preceded by a blank line that runs the length of the page. The action element is responsible for setting the scene, literally, as it describes the setting. In it you will introduce what your characters are doing in the scene that will ideally naturally set the scene for what is going to come next. Any action written in this section should be written in real time, which means you are going to want to write as crisply and cleanly as possible in an effort to convey exactly what the audience will see on screen.

When you write your action elements, it is important to leave out as many extraneous details as possible as this makes the script easier to shoot as fewer unique props will be required. The only time you are going to want to go over the top with atmospheric descriptions is when the atmosphere is crucial to what is taking place on screen. For example, if you picture your favorite horror movie, you can bet that the scene that introduced the main location contain an action element with descriptive text.

However, if you are writing scenes that include lots of tense, back and forth dialogue, or action, then you are going to want to do your best to ensure descriptions are kept to an overall minimum. This will help to create an overall feeling of watching the scene play out in real time which naturally makes your script feel as though it could easily be adapted to the big screen.

In order to write action that plays on the page, the easiest thing to do is picture yourself having coffee with a friend and discussing something interesting you saw on your way to the café. This way you will be sure that you cut out all the filler and only focus on the parts that really matter. During these scenes, you are going to want to keep your paragraphs short, no more than five lines in a paragraph, no matter what. Be sure to capitalize any sound effects that are used. Between each paragraph you are going to want to leave two blank lines. By splitting up your descriptions and your action, you are adding an overall visual emphasis to your story, making it feel more like a movie throughout.

When introducing characters, capitalize the entire name, you are also going to want to include a specific gender as well as age. This information is not only going to be crucial when it comes to understanding what is going on in the story, but when it comes to things like budgeting and casting as well. Make sure you don't go so far as to describe specific hairstyles and clothing, except in situations where it is crucial to the plot. You are also going to want to avoid using parenthesis to indicate action when introducing a character. This means no: BOB (cracks a beer).

When describing movement, you are going to never want to use the word camera. Instead, replace it with the word we. This means no: the camera follows, instead it would be: we follow…

Setting up dialogue: The name of the character who is speaking is going to appear in all caps, tabbed in to almost the center of the page and then directly followed by relevant dialogue. The name of the person speaking can either be the name of the character (BOB) or a description if the person isn't known (MAN IN BLACK). Occupations are also acceptable if they are easily identifiable by the average person. If a character is going to play more than an incidental role in the story they should have a name. Be consistent when you refer to a named character, this means no calling BOB by his name in once scene and then by his last name in the next.

Writing Dialogue: The dialogue itself is going to appear located between the left margin, which is where the slug and the action are written and the margin where the character name is written. Writing good dialogue is certainly an art form all to itself, and most new screenwriters make the mistake of over-writing their dialogue.

The end result of this, in most cases is going to be dialogue that comes off more like a play than a movie, which tends to make scenes seem slower than they might otherwise be. It is important to try and keep your dialogue informal, while at the same time not stuffing it full of as much slang as you can manage. If it is important to the story that you character have a regional dialect, you can mention it when you describe them initially, but do not write out their lines in a regional dialect, unless it is a single line written in such a way to indicate emphasis.

When writing dialogue, it is important to make an effort to reflect the personality of each character in the things that they say, while also walking a fine line of not overdoing it. This will make it easier for the reader to picture the conversation as if it were actually happening, as opposed to two characters in a book, spouting soliloquies at one another. This also relates to the way in which key information is relied by the characters in the scenes. You should aim to express inner feelings in a subtle manner, without resorting to on the nose writing where each character simply says what they are thinking or feeling. Your overall goal should be to make the reader, and thus ultimately the audience, feel as though they are a fly on the wall for a real conversation.

Keep in mind that during almost all conversations, the primary players are rarely going to come right out and say whatever it is they mean. Instead, the conversation is going to have subtext. This means you are going to want to leave out bits and pieces of what exactly is going on and allow the audience the opportunity to figure it out on their own. Not only will this make the scene feel more natural, it will be more interesting to watch (or read) as well. For example, in the movie Jerry Maguire, the character of Jerry Maguire uses the phrase "You complete me" to indicate that he is finally ready to express his feelings for the romantic lead. In this instance, the audience knows he means he loves her because earlier in the movie there was a scene of a deaf couple using sign language and a discussion of the sign for love.

While this example is just a little thing, it still makes the audience think, which is a key to keeping them interested in what is taking place in front of them. As such, you are going to want to consider every line of dialogue that you write and the other possible ways that the same intent could be expressed without directly coming right out and saying it.

Parenthetical information: Any parenthetical information that you need to include in your script is going to appear left indented within brackets, underneath the character name. They are used only to express the emotion the character is currently feeling in the moment. For example, (laughing), (angry), or (upset). Any parenthetical information you provide should always be short, descriptive and to the point. As with any ancillary information, they should only be used when they are crucial to the plot.

Transition elements: Certain transitions are going to be optional, these include things like DISSOLVE TO: or CUT TO:. When you use them, they are going to need to be right indented, not flush right, and should only come after a blank line on the page and should always be followed by two blank lines as well. When you come to the end of page without completing a scene, the scene transition should always stay with the shot that was just completed which means you will never start a new page with either DISSOLVE TO: or CUT TO:, those would remain at the bottom of the previous page.

Transitions are primarily used to denote a major shift in time or location, and sometimes, like using MATCH CUT TO:, for effect. You are generally going to want to leave out transition any time you find yourself rapidly cutting between scenes when adding them in will noticeably disrupt the flow of the sequence in question. This is particularly true for chase or montage scenes.

Chapter 2: Television Screenwriting Considerations

The format for television shows differs depending on how long they are supposed to run. Hour-long dramas are written up much like a movie screenplay, however, there are always breaks for act changes. Meanwhile, sitcoms and other, shorter, television shows are written a little differently which means their scripts have different formats to discern what they are supposed to be. The biggest difference between television and movie screenplays is that the level of standardization between genres, or even varying shows is far less well-defined. There are still going to have some hard and fast rules, however, which means the first thing you are going to want to do before you write a spec script is to read several scripts for the show you are going to be writing for so that you get a feel for what makes it unique.

Nevertheless, there are going to be some similarities in this field as well, and it is important that you understand what they are to ensure you get off on the right foot. One thing that is never going to change is the structure of the show in question. A 30-

minute television show is 22 minutes of content and 8 minutes of advertising (in general) and an hourlong show is typically 45 minutes of content and 15 minutes of commercials. The breaks need to be located in the right spots, which means the act breaks, with two or three additional breaks, depending on the network, for hourlong shows.

Drama

When it comes to writing drama, a good rule of thumb is to start every scene already in progress and make sure to move on to the next too early as opposed to too late. Additionally, you are going to want to be extremely selective when it comes to the scenes you do include, each one will need to either develop your characters or advance your plot, there is little room for anything else. The scenes that are going to end on commercial breaks should end on points of high dramatic tension, even if it is not integral to the plot as a whole. Above all you are going to want to keep your focus on showing, rather than telling.

Common types of dramas: There are several major types of dramas that tend to get produced, this is not to say that nothing else is ever going to get on the air, they are just the evergreen types of shows you can always expect to find somewhere on the dial. The first is the procedural, while this was once largely classified to police shows, there are now countless variations on the traditional solve a mystery in an hour formula, and you can find everything from medical to supernatural procedurals on television these days. The next type is the workplace drama, where there is equal focus on the jobs the characters do as well as on their personal lives.

After the success of *Game of Thrones*, the genre drama went from a small niche to big business. These types of shows typically blend fantasy or science fiction with more grounded characters and interpersonal stories. Finally, there are dramas found on premium cable channels, which can fall into any of the categories, but typically deal in much more extreme content matter and also don't need to worry about the traditional act breaks found in non-premium scripts.

Formatting: When it comes to formatting an hourlong script, if you don't have any sample material to look at, you can safely assume that it will be formatted in the same way a feature script would be, more or less, with the biggest difference being the act breaks. Don't forget, the average page of script is assumed to be about one minute, and the average script tends to come in at no more than 60 pages.

The first page, the cover page, that you provide should include the name of the show above the title of the episode above the writer's name. The next page will be the title name and it should include the same information as the cover page as well as your contact information printed below it.

The average episode is broken up into a teaser, which sets the stage for the episode and is what the viewer will see before the title sequence. The rest of the script will then be broken into four acts. Again, this is only an estimate as there are numerous shows that alter this format in one way or another, the best choice is always going to be tracking down a sample script from the show in question if you hope to be taken seriously.

Each act is going to be given a numerical designation and center at the top of the page that starts the act. Broadly speaking, both Act One and Act 1 are acceptable, just ensure that you are consistent throughout. Likewise, the end of each act should by bookended by End Act _. This should be two lines below the final line of text from the act, bolded and centered. FADE or CUT may be used to end a scene, but this is not required. A simple scene slug will do instead. Each new act should then start fresh at the top of a new page.

The average page breakdown per section works out as follows

Teaser: Between two and four pages

Act one: Between 14 and 15 pages

Act two: Between 14 and 15 pages

Act three: Between 14 and 15 pages

Act four: Between 14 and 15 pages

Tag: Between one and two pages

Total: Between 59 and 66 pages

Narrative structure: Broadly speaking, you are going to want to follow a standard three act structure for your script, the first act should set up the goal for the episode and the end of the first act will generally end with them failing to reach some sort of instant gratification. The second act will further complicate whatever it is that the main character is trying to do, while simultaneously raising the stakes. The end of this act will find the character at their lowest point for the entire episode.

Act three typically begins with something that renews the character's resolve and pushes them to get right to the point where they are going to attempt to overcome their obstacle. Finally, act four resolves everything, though the amount to which this is the case is going to be determined by whether or not the episodes are designed for standalone or serialized viewing.

As a general rule, you can expect the average modern series to include the main plot as well as two subplots that all take place at the same time. The main story is the A plot, the B plot is then the more involved of the two subplots while the C plot, also known as the runner, is typically limited to character building moments. These typically occur about three times throughout the episode. If your subplots are going to be referencing specific details from other plotlines of the television show in question, you will need to indicate where in the series continuity it takes place on the title page.

Sitcoms

The first thing you need to understand about writing situation comedies, is that you already need to be adept at telling jokes in order to succeed in the medium. Specifically, you need to concern yourself with timing as if a joke is executed poorly, especially on the page without a comedic actor to save it, it will fall flat every time.

Multicamera: When considering writing a sitcom script, the first thing you will need to consider is if the show you are considering writing a script for is filmed in the multicamera or single camera mindset. In general, you can expect a multicamera shows to have two acts while single camera shows will more often have three.

The general format for a multicamera show is as follows:

FADE IN: this should always be written in capital letters and underlined.

SCENE the scene should be numbered, capitalized and underlined with two spaces above and below it.

Slug the slug should always be underlined .

(Character list) the character list should be written directly underneath the slug and is used to tell the reader which characters are going to be in the scene. It should be encapsulated inside a parenthesis.

DESCRIPTIONS AND ACTIONS both required actions and relevant descriptions are always capitalized, don't forget to keep these to only plot specific requirements.

CHARACTER INTROS this should always be written in capital letters and underlined.

CAMERA INSTRUCTIONS, SPECIAL EFFFECTS AND SOUND EFFECTS this should always be written in capital letters and underlined.

CHARACTER NAMES AND DIALOUGE these should always be written in capital letters and double spaced.

(PERSONAL DIRECTION) this will appear within lines of dialogue, in all capital letters and enclosed in a parenthesis.

The first page after the cover and title page of average sitcom script will start with the name of the show written in capital letters, exactly six lines down from the top of the page and surrounded by quotation marks. Six lines below this you will want to center ACT ONE followed by A on the next line, which indicates the scene, also centered. 8 lines underneath this you will then write FADE IN: so that it aligns with a 1.4-inch margin. This should be followed by the list of characters that is going to appear in the scene. Each page should be numbered and also include the letter corresponding to the scene in question.

The second scene, and each additional scene will then start on a new page. 21 lines down from the top of the page you will put the scene designation, centered. Six lines below that you will then write the slug. Each act will also begin on a new page. When you are writing dialogue, you are going to want to make it double spaced to ensure it is easy to read. When you write stage direction, ensure you do so in all capital letters in order to more easily distinguish them from the dialogue. Each page should contain plenty of white space to ensure actors have space to write their own notes. In general, the following page breakdown should apply.

Teaser: Between one and two pages

Act one: Between 13 and 20 pages, depending on if the story has two or three acts

Act two: Between 13 and 20 pages, depending on if the story has two or three acts

Act three: Between 0 and 13 pages, depending on if the story has two or three acts

Tag: Between one and three pages

Total: Between 40 and 48 pages

Single camera: Single camera shows are typically going to be formatted more like dramas, though again, specific shows may vary. Even if they have commercial breaks, they may not have a traditional three act structure, especially if the entire season is serialized. When writing dialogue, as well as stage direction, you are going to want to make sure that both are single-spaced. Additionally, each character should have their name written in all capital letters the first time they are introduced onscreen. These scripts are typically the tightest of the three, rarely coming in at more than 32 pages in length.

Additional Tips to Keep In Mind

When writing for a sitcom, above all else you need to nail the tone as well as the voice of each character on the show you are writing a script for. The people who will be reading spec scripts know their shows inside and out and they will respond better to those they can tell know it just as well.

Your spec script should be thought of as your portfolio, resume and calling card all in one. As such, you better make sure it is great if you ever hope to get your foot in the door. In addition to being a tight, well-written story, your script needs to be completely free of all errors, if grammar isn't your strong suit, get someone else to edit your script for you. A lack of concern over the little things won't reflect well overall and could easily be the deciding factor between you and another aspiring screenwriter.

In general, you are going to want to stay away from writing a pilot before you have even landed a job in the industry as pilots from unknowns are rarely picked up. With that being said, however, if you have a great idea for a show, write the pilot episode and then write two or three more. By this point your characters will be more well-established and you can show the reader what your average episode is going to be like. This is crucial as the early episodes of many shows are spent establishing character relationships and interactions, leaving less time for traditional activities and jokes and leading to scripts that seem limp.

Avoid using parentheticals whenever possible. Only leave them in if they clearly enhance the dialogue in a specific way. One of the only acceptable times is when the parenthetical will explain body language that will indicate that the character is saying one thing while clearly meaning something else. Likewise, you are going to want to avoid unnecessary explanations, if you can't make the scene work without explaining it, you should cut it, period. Finally, avoid adding scenes just to fill space, if you can fill out a full-length script with useful content it's time to go back to the drawing board.

Chapter 3: How to Create Characters

When it comes to writing a compelling screenplay, the first thing you that is likely going to come to you is going to be the basic outline of the plot. In order to ensure that this basic idea matures organically into a fully fleshed-out screenplay, the first thing you are going to want to do is more fully consider the characters that are going to be going with you on the adventure you are creating. You will find that getting to know your characters more intimately will make the process of actually connecting the dots on the story much more manageable.

You are not just going to want to only focus on creating a protagonist, you are going to want to consider who are going to be the main characters of your story, both protagonists and antagonists, and write character biographies as well. In fact, this is encouraged, especially if you are writing a feature length screenplay. You want a solid backstory and a solid foundation for writing your character into your story. This is a great way to create a very strong character that will draw the audience's attention until the very end.

Always remember the Theory of Illumination. This theory states that every character reflects on your main character. Their relationships, and their development, eventually lead them to your main character. While giving every character a fully-developed backstory on screen is not recommended, knowing the details of a character's life will make them easier to write for in addition to making them seem more well-rounded as a whole.

This means that you aren't going to want to flesh out all of your character bios in a single evening, you need to spend some time to really think each of your characters through. Take a few days where you spend a few hours to think about your characters, this time should be spent without distractions. No phones, no TV, no music, just you and your thoughts, because you want your character to be authentic, not a copy of a distraction that sticks in your mind. You want a truly original person, not a second-rate copy of someone else's character.

Then, you just start writing. Write anything that you feel is relevant to your character's development. Just let your character grow, and pretty much create themselves, with only the manipulation of the outline you have decided on. This is called free association. Free associating is where you let the words take you wherever, and you merely go along for the ride. This allows you to ensure that your character is not too stiff. You want your character to be real, not forced.

This is not say that everything you write during this period is going to be usable, and indeed much of it may be garbage. However, if you can successfully manage to channel your character for this process you never know what useful information you may end up discovering.

You want to follow every major aspect of your character, true, but you cannot neglect the small things that add up to make your character truly who they are. Remember, people are not made up of only the defining moments in their lives, they are also made up of all of the little, seemingly insignificant moments inbetween. You could possibly do a portion where you outline what their day looks like from the time they wake up, to the time they go to sleep. This will help you better establish the type of person your character will be as well.

If you find an area in your character's life, and you are not sure exactly which way to proceed, let the cards fall where they may. If you are still unsure, do a little research, and go from there. You want to know everything about your character, but you can also be surprised where the words take you. Remember, if you don't like what you come up with you can always scrap it later. When writing your script you should only be focused on creating the best story possible, not with how long the process takes you.

Write! Do not worry about if other people will love it, because if you do not, then no one will. You have to first and foremost be able to stand behind your screenplay one hundred percent. Otherwise, it will not be taken seriously. As the quality of your overall screenplay is going to be dependent on the strength of your characters, it equally stands to reason that you need to love them first, before you worry about anything else.

It is important to create dynamic characters and to keep yourself in line with how you want your screenplay to go. The character has to fall in line with what you want to achieve, and yet they also have to bring a certain element to the table as well. They have to create a little bit of chaos, while also maintaining the peace so to speak.

Imagine you are walking a tightrope. You have to have precision balance. That is what making a character is like. You have to have some flaws as no one wants to root for a character that is perfect. However, too many flaws will make your character seem like a mess, and unless your character is actually a mess, you want them to be relatable. So, you have to walk that tightrope between peace and chaos. This is harder than most people think. As it becomes too easy to make a character extremely flawed, or completely perfect. It becomes too easy to fall to one side or the other, and you have to stay in the middle. It is okay to teeter a few times, but you have to pull your balance back up and continue on.

If you are not able to do so, you will find that the whole story veers out of control, and that can make your screenplay less than desirable. This is what you want to avoid for a plethora of reasons, but the first being that you

Here are my top 5 tips for writing stronger characters into your screenplay:

Make your character likable early on: You have to make your character someone that the audience wants to spend at least ninety minutes with. This means you have to make them likable from the get-go. Even if you think the character is interesting, if they are not very positive, or they are annoying, the audience will lose interest before you get to the good parts of the character.

You want the audience to be able to identify with the character because that is what draws their interest in. The main character should be written as the protagonist, this way the main person is not a self-serving, negative drawback to the screenplay, unless the entire purpose of the screenplay is to chronicle their downfall or their redemption. In general, however, people want to see the negative characters portrayed as the antagonist. This way there is some balance between good and bad though, typically, good will win out in the end.

Your character does not have to be perfect, they just have to have some redeeming qualities. These qualities will help your character reach out to the audience in a way that keeps them interested. You can do this by making the dialogue witty and conversational. You can make them do a kind act in the beginning, such as saving a cat from a tree. In fact, there is an entire screenwriting book, entitled *Save the Cat* for just that reason. Regardless of the setup you choose, you just have to make sure that you set the tone for a likable character early on in the story. This is important, because if you do not, you may find that you lose your audience's interest before even grabbing a hold of it properly.

If you have a character that maybe does not have the best qualities, then it is important to include other, worse, characters to make him seem better in comparison. For example, if you have a character that may be in prison, you want to make him better than the other prisoners. Your character does not have to be a saint, just better than the others, and more relatable than a villain. They have to have a sense of purpose about them, to attract the audience to the plot line, and help them retain their interest until the very end. A complex character cannot get lost in his flaws.

Build realistic & detailed characters: While the character is who your person is, characterization is what they are. One is the true deep soul of the character, the other is the shallower, facade that they present to the rest of the world. For example, you could have a lonely woman who just wants someone to love as a character, but her characterization could be a CEO of a company who acts like she does not need anything from anyone. This is characterization. Sometimes the two are similar, and sometimes they are polar opposites. Like a hard, edgy teen is truly a softy on the inside. These contrasts, when revealed, make for a more detailed, believable characters, and a better storyline. People love to be surprised and love finding out more about the characters in a story. So, you have to make sure that you detail their characterization precisely. You want to make sure that you put some emphasis on who they are, but also what they are as well – the inside and the outside.

Writing strong characterization is important on so many levels. First off, a realistically depicted character will add a lot of realism to your piece. I cannot count how many times I've seen the same generic antagonist in a film that had zero original characterization, which ultimately completely diminished their importance in the film. But even outside of just adding realism to the characters, it can also help you as a writer to tell your story more intuitively and dramatically.

Just like you want to write a character biography, you also want to create characterization sheets. These help you discern what your character will be like throughout most of the screenplay. You can do this quickly, through another round of free association. Give your character choices, as if they were living, breathing, individuals. It is important for you to be free flowing with your characters so that they feel authentic and realistic. If you try to force your character to completely match someone who inspires you, the character will feel forced. Let the character speak to you. Which, coincidentally, brings us directly up to the next tip.

Let your character make the decisions for you: Many writers feel that their screenplay has to be completely mapped out before they even begin writing, and while it is important for you to make sure that you have the structure outlined, it is equally important to let your characters breathe, otherwise the setting will feel fake and forced, which is the opposite of what you want.

Rather than forcing your character into a box that you have neatly outlined before you have even touched the first sentence, you should let your character make their own decisions. This may sound silly because you are the writer, but the truth is, once you have spent enough time with your characters this will seem much more reasonable. Once you have spent enough time chronicling their likes and dislikes, you will find that you will be able to easily picture what they would do when confronted with a specific decision. You want them to come alive and come off the page, which means you have to let the characters take control sometimes. This allows the scene to feel more realistic, and give it more depth.

While your character may be an extension of yourself, they are also a separate entity from you as well and should be treated as such. With that being said, however, if you give a character a trait that you share with them, then it becomes much easier to anticipate how they would act in a given situation as you can use your own experiences as a point of reference.

If you have already created a character biography and a characterization sheet, then this should be an easy thing to do. You should know your character inside out, and as your character grows, how they will make their way through the story should become clear. So, while you might have thought the character could go one way, you may be surprised when you get to that point, and find that another solution suddenly makes more sense.

Likewise, you are going to want your characters to grow organically which means letting them change as the story dictates, as opposed to forcing them to remain in a predetermined box. Not only will this do a disservice to the character overall, it is unsatisfying for an audience to leave a character exactly where they started, either mentally, emotionally or physically, unless that fact is central to the overall plot. You want them to be like real people, because they will be portrayed by real people, and your target audience will be real people, so you have to make sure that your character has depth.

Approach the early drafts with an open mind, and that will help you build an organic, relatable character. Even if it means you have to change a lot because one choice changes everything.

You will find that the more you let your character choose, the more realistic the story will feel, and the more interest the story will garner. This is what you are looking for because you want the character to draw the audience in. It is important that you write some serious choices in as well, as a screenplay without real consequences is likely lacking in dramatic tension as well.

Give your character compelling dialogue: Dialogue was touched on earlier, but it is important enough to warrant further consideration. All of your characters need to have a strong dialogue. This will establish who they are within their first few lines. Even if they do not have a lot of lines, the ones that they have should be solid, and discerning.

So much can be conveyed by the simple use of dialogue. Accent can determine where the character is from. Their sentence structure can determine how educated they are. The tone of voice can determine if they are introverted or extroverted. All of this and more can be shown just by how the character's lines are written.

Something as simple as a scene where a character is running errands, and talking to the people they meet can tell a lot about the character. This may seem odd, but it is true because they are showing a piece of themselves in their everyday life.

Even though the narrative films are fiction, people want them to seem as realistic as they possibly can. This is because people like what they can relate to. They want to be able to feel a connection to a character, even if it is an animated character. Dialogue is a great way to do that.

Compelling dialogue is not always a lot of dialogue. You could have a character that speaks very little, and yet they could be a very dynamic character. How you set up their dialogue really sets the tone for how they are portrayed. You have to make sure that no matter how many lines of dialogue a character has, they are set up to portray a depth to that character.

Something that you want to stay away from is one-dimensional dialogue. This is where all of your characters speak the same. Even if they are all from the same area and same family, every person speaks differently. While similar characters may have similar dialogue, they should also have their own unique characteristics in their dialogue. This will help you discern the different people when the storyline starts speeding up. If you have all the same dialogue, the characters will blend into one another.

#5 – Think like an actor and give your character a point of view

One of the most important things to think about is the character's point of view. As the writer, you see everything, but the main character does not. You have to make sure that you are writing with the character's point of view to ensure that confusion does not set in by the character knowing something that would be impossible for them to know. This clutters things up and makes it hard to keep the scenes straight.

If you are laughing at this tip, you need it the most. You cannot just slap a character down all willy-nilly, you have to put some thought into it. You want a character that will be easy to figure out so that the actor can do the character the justice they deserve.

The most important reason to write a strong point of view is that it gives a line for the story to follow. The audience needs to understand where the character stands, and if the character does not have a solid point of view, then this gets harder to do, and it gets frustrating for the audience, the actors, and everyone involved in the creation of the work you have worked so hard on.

Have you ever seen *Forrest Gump?* In the movie, the main character, Forrest Gump, has a very strong point of view. In fact, the entire movie is told from his point of view. You can see where he stands on life, love, and running. This is what you are looking for in a character, even if it is not written in first person point of view.

There are so many screenplays that lack this concept. These are the ones that often get tossed out because no one wants to be confused for ninety minutes. They want to be able to easily follow the character.

Some scenes are drawn out longer than necessary because the character does not have a strong point of view, which causes the scenes to run around in circles. This makes it harder to follow, and more confusing for the audiences that you may have.

A test to see if you are heading in the right direction is to see if you could cut the scene down to no more than two pages. While some scenes need a lot of dialogue, there are still ways to cut it down to make those two pages, and if you cannot do that, then perhaps you have to reevaluate the scene and the character's strength in their point of view. It is best to do this in the editing stages to see what needs to be changed.

What else can we do?

There is no set formula for how to write a character, but if you follow these tips, you will be off to a good start. It is important that you find what works for you because you have to have a solid character for your storyline to move forward.

In fact, all of your characters need to be strong, so that they move the story along smoothly. A bad character is like a speed bump. It interrupts a steady pace and can be frustrating if there is a lot of them.

There are other tips that you can find from other writers as well. Spend some time with your local writer's guild, or go to the library. This will help you immensely to find yourself and find the character you are looking to create. You have to have a solid grasp on your character, for them to flourish.

Go out in the world, and people watch. You can get some ideas for character traits you would like to have in a character. Walmart, the mall, the park. These are all great places to find interesting characters.

Chapter 4: Creating a Rough Draft

Most contracts that you enter into will give you three months maximum from the pitch to come up with a rough draft. Three months may seem like a good amount of time, but it is actually not a lot of time. You have to work swiftly, and efficiently to get your rough draft out in time. Otherwise, you may lose your shot.

Something that helps is to remember that screenplays are time-related. While a novel can be as long or as short as you would like, most feature films run between ninety minutes and two hours. This makes it harder, and easier at the same time. It gives you an idea of how many pages to write but also makes it that much more restrictive to write with a deadline, and a page limit as well. You want to make sure that you streamline the process, to make things go a lot easier.

Getting a good workflow will give you a good storyline. You do not want to seem like you rushed the development. Here are some ideas for a good workflow.

Develop the story idea:

Before you can come up with a story, you must first start with an idea. You cannot just slap words on a page and call it a screenplay. Go somewhere that inspires you, and get an idea for the story from start to finish.

Create the pitch:

Then you have to create the pitch that will give you an idea of how the story will flow. Start with the five finger pitch. This is where you list some major events on one hand. These events once explained should flow nicely. If they do not go do some more thinking. If they do, then you can move on to the two-handed pitch which is just more events that flow smoothly. Once this is complete, you have a solid foundation for your storyline.

Give it structure:

This is like adding the walls to a house. You have to add more turning points, and supporting events. You want to be able to hold the story up, and by giving it structure, then you can have a full blown story coming your way soon.

The importance of structure is that it keeps the entire story from just falling apart at the seams. If you do not have a strong structure of your house, it will fall down. Same with a story.

Build a full story:

Also known as a synopsis, this is where you get all of the major events mapped out. Basically, the synopsis is a one page summary of the entire story. It is the story without all of the minor details and dialogue. Once this is done, you can move onto the next step, which brings you closer to actually writing the rough draft.

Create a beat sheet:

This is a basic outline that will help you keep track of where the story is at, and where it will go next. The outline does not need to be really detailed, it is just a little bullet point list that you can check off as you pass each point in your writing once you finally get to writing your script.

The importance of a beat sheet is to ensure that you are keeping up with the storyline, and moving at the proper pace. Otherwise, you will find that you are stuck, and being stuck can cost you precious time.

Write the script (finally):

Woohoo! It is finally time to get to script writing. You have to make sure that your outline is complete first, and then you can get down to business. There are a lot of software out there that will help you, as they already have the formatting ready for you. Some also have tips and tricks for writing a good script as well. If you are not sure of your abilities, there are software out there that will proofread your script as well for you, though they are a little more costly.

As you are writing, you may find that you need to tweak what you had previously written. Do not go deleting anything yet, instead, create a list of things that need to be fixed, and when you go to edit your rough draft afterward, then you can create an edited rough draft later on. This way you can keep things on track, and get your first rough draft punched out.

Do not delete your original rough draft. It should be kept as your first draft in case you need to go back and reference changes. Once you have edited all of the additional things into your script, you can celebrate.

NEXT STEPS:

The next step is to get your rough draft to the company you have a contract with. They will look it over, and tell you if they like it, and what they feel needs work. Then you can get to editing.

Chapter 5: Editing a Screenplay

Have you ever wondered why a character is rarely seen eating, drinking water, or going to the bathroom unless it has significance to the storyline? The reason these things are rarely portrayed is that this would be too much information, and would drag the story on too long.

In any storytelling form, you have to edit the life of a character in some way. This will keep the storyline moving, and keep it from getting tedious. Bathroom breaks, minor incidences, and repetitive action are generally not important in a storyline, so if you have too much of these, they should be edited out.

Before a screenplay is produced, there are many ways a writer can edit their screenplays. Whether it be through editing and rearranging scenes, juxtaposition, and cutting the fat. All of these are resources that will help the editing process move forward.

Juxtaposition is important to use in any form of art, and screenwriting does not escape its grasp. Just by changing the juxtaposition of scenes, you can give the story an entirely different feel.

This can be used in one scene or two scenes, or depending on how many you need to use it on to help get the point across.

Crosscut and parallel action are two points of juxtaposition that are most commonly used in writing, and they are found to be very effective in creating different tones for different scenes, which is what writers want to achieve.

For instance, a very fun moment cut directly into a boring moment can accentuate that boredom through contrast.

Juxtaposition is a word that is not overlooked in any editing class. It is useful in so many areas, from writing to cinematography, and stage preparation. Prop work as well. The contrast it creates can be useful in setting a tone and creating a mood. This makes it less necessary for words to set the tone, which will leave you more words for important things.

Sometimes, you get so attached to your story that you do not want to cut anything, but the unnecessary parts are important to cut because they just slow the production down. It is important to cut them before they get to production if possible because you do not want to waste more time than you absolutely have to.

Some directors are more spontaneous though. They want you to leave it all in, and they will see how it works as it is being filmed. However, if you cannot get a scene to work when you are writing it, it is still best to leave it out.

However, if you are lower budget, you should make all of the necessary cuts before production, because any delays can cost a lot of money. If you do not have that much money, to begin with, then you will have a hard time recovering.

Removing weaker scenes do not just help production, they help the budget as well. Every page of the script costs money, and if you cut the weaker scenes that wouldn't make the cut anyway, then you save the money it would take to produce them.

Cutting scenes post-production also causes a lot of problems with continuity in a piece as well, because there is not enough time to smooth out the edges.

The continuity of a film is really important. Without that continuity, it will feel like someone gave a twelve-year-old a camera and told them to make a movie.

It is important to take the lighting into consideration as well. Consider how the light will affect the mood. So when editing, you have to pay close attention to the lighting to make sure it stays consistent. Fix it if you need to because the wrong lighting could set the wrong mood, which would shut your whole production down. If you do not want that you will make sure to specify the time of day in every scene.

Not only does the light change, but your character may also change as well. If a lot of time progresses, your character cannot stay the same the entire time. You have to make sure that you have made note of the changes as the film progresses.

The visuals are usually clear-cut, but if scenes need to be cut in post-production, that can disrupt the visuals. If several scenes need cut, then you may find that certain scenes need to be reshot to fix the visuals. This is another reason to focus on editing closely.

When editing, it is important to keep in mind the order of the scenes to ensure that the continuity is there. If something needs to be switched around, make sure to adjust it accordingly, so that the visuals are smooth, and there are no visual speed bumps when you hit production. Because it becomes a lot harder to fix on the spot then, and you want a smooth transition to have a successful film. Visuals are very important, and it is important to remember that.

Another part of editing is to make sure that you note the transitions. Every film has to have transitions between scenes so that they flow smoothly. Otherwise, you would have to add a whole lot more information. These transitions are a lot easier to add in the editing process than the post-production days. So make sure to make a note of the transitions before it becomes harder to add them.

Another reason to make sure everything is solid in editing is that there can be unwanted interpretations if you have to cut scenes in post-production. Doing so between similar scenes can create confusion, and doing so between contrasting scenes can be jarring and dramatic. This can be used to say something if it is intentional. However, if it is not intentional, you risk saying something to the audience that you never meant to say, which can leave them confused.

Also, directors do not like to be told how to do their job, so avoid technical directions in your script. Instead be subtle in telling the director where the camera should be pointed. Instead of saying "Point camera to the west." You could say "The main character looked off into a beautiful sunset, contemplating the meaning of life. Since the sun sets in the west, the camera will point west.

Editing can save you from a lot of issues later on in life and ensures smoother transitions as you head into production. It is important to make sure you edit out all of the kinks to save money when it comes time to shoot the film. Now if only taxes could be edited out of our lives.

Chapter 6: Tips for Success

While there are a wide variety of reasons that you might want to be a screenwriter, if you are hoping to do so in order to adopt a shorter, less stressful, work week you may be extremely disappointed. In fact, successful screenwriters are often extremely disciplined, dedicated individuals who have trained themselves to create something from nothing, day end and day out in order to ensure they always have something productive in the pipeline. While what works out to be an effective process for each writer is going to differ, sometimes dramatically, the most successful all typically have a number of habits in common that make the task before them more manageable. These are outlined here, in hopes that at least a few of them will inspire you to write more successfully in the future.

They have a reason to write: The best screenplays, especially those written by first time screenwriters are written with a specific purpose in mind, by writers with a driving desire to tell a specific story. This doesn't mean that your motivations for telling your story need to be pure as the driven snow, after all, entertaining others is as good of reason as any. The important thing is that you have a reason that is strong enough to drive you to continue trying to tell your story no matter how hard the going is going to get, and it is likely to be quite difficult from time to time.

Regardless of the motives that you have for writing, you need to be passionate about it if you ever hope to find true success. Don't feel ashamed if part of the reason that you want to write a successful screenplay has something to do with egotism, remember, the goal isn't to make yourself want to write a screenplay that will change the world, it is to find what drives you to write, and in this case egotism is as useful of a reason as any. Everyone wants recognition to some degree, and if you want to write for revenge, glory, fame, money, power, or simply to prove that you can, then you can harness that energy and use to make you a better writer, ensuring you actually see the screenplay through in the process.

They demand the best from themselves: When you first start writing your screenplay, it is perfectly acceptable to leave in placeholder scenes and text, from time to time, just to ensure you make it through to the end in one piece. With that being said, it is important to keep in mind that the spec script your produce is going to be the one, and often only, thing that people in the industry look at when they decide if they are going to give you your big break which means that settling for anything less that absolute perfection is akin to throwing away all the time that you ultimately spend on your screenplay.

As such, it is important to never settle with your first draft, your second or even your fourth. You are going to want to go through the entire thing with a fine-tooth comb until the story is as tight and compelling as possible. While this is only going to ever take you so far, it will at least ensure that the screenplay that you send in is the most accurate indication of what you are capable of as possible.

At the same time, you are going to want to make a conscious effort to stop making changes at the point where the work, as presented, speaks for itself as you can always find something to tweak or change. Eventually you are going to need to have the confidence in yourself to put the work out there and, hopefully, start receiving feedback on it. If you don't practice restraint, your screenplay will likely end up feeling overwrought, as you will have overthought whatever spark was there to begin with into oblivion.

They write what they like, and what they know: While anyone can have an idea for any type of story, and that story might be unique, or relatable, enough to resonate with the world at large, you will typically find that it is much easier to write about things that you have first-hand knowledge about and also much easier to keep at it if you like whatever it is that you are writing. Again, it is perfectly acceptable to get into the screenwriting business for its potential for lucrative gains, this in no way means that you can't enjoy the process along the way. What's more, if you find the story in your screenplay exciting, the odds are high that those around you are going to feel the same way.

Likewise, when it comes to writing what you know, this doesn't mean writing a movie about being an accountant for an accounting firm, unless you have an idea that will make the process seem roughly 2,000 percent more exciting than the topic naturally seems to the average person. Rather, adding in touches from your every day life can make certain characters more believable, or giving one of your hobbies to a character can make them seem more three-dimensional. What's more, you never know when something from, even a seemingly boring job, can provide you with the one realistic, but unexpected, fact that you need to tie the whole plot together.

They set goals: If you have never before found yourself sitting in front of a blank screen, with all the freedom in the world in front of you, only to find yourself looking for any excuse to be anywhere else, then the idea of setting writing goals to ensure you actually finish your screenplay may seem unnecessary. The first time you make the decision to bolt rather than face down your writer's block, however, you will realize just how vital setting goals can be. Likewise, if you have never written anything substantial before, then you may find yourself doing all the research you need to complete your screenplay, only to find that you never actually get any closer to generating a truly finished product.

As such, you should start by setting goals for your pre-writing process, including generating characters, a basic plot synopsis, world building elements etc. You should give yourself plenty of time for the more free-form nature of this part of the process, though you should have a firm deadline when you want to begin the actual writing to ensure that fleshing out your characters doesn't end up taking years to finish.

When it comes to writing the first draft, you are going to want to make a concentrated effort to write for at least an hour a day, at least five days a week, and also spend some time on the sixth day coming up with a general idea of where the end of the next week should find you. Writing every day will help to ensure that you don't lose the flow of the story as it can be hard to recapture lost momentum once it has slipped away. While writing for a set period of time is fine, you will find that you will be more productive still if you task yourself with writing a set number of pages each day. This will ensure that you maintain your productivity, rather than just waiting out the clock on days where inspiration takes longer to strike. In addition to page goals, you are going to want to have a general idea of where you want to the story to go next, so you can steer things in that direction.

When it comes to editing, you are going to want to set hourly goals, as it is difficult to say just how much work you will get done per session as it is going to vary so dramatically. When it comes to setting an overall timeline for completion, you are going to want to give yourself enough time to ensure you don't rush, but not so much that you don't feel obligated to make daily progress. When setting these goals, it is important to keep in mind that they are not taking place in a vacuum. Writing for three or four hours every day is an admirable goal, and likely one that is completely unrealistic if you already have a fulltime job. It is important to set goals that are achievable as failing to do so can harm your morale and making finishing your screenplay harder than it already is.

Finally, the overall length of your timeline isn't important, as there is no standard amount of time it should take to create a quality screenplay. The most important thing overall, is that setting a schedule will help you to make finishing your screenplay a priority which means you are going to be far more likely to finish it than you otherwise would. Remember, your screenplay could be your shot at the bigtime, but the only way you will ever know for sure is if you actually finish it.

Conclusion

Hopefully, you learned a lot about writing a screenplay from this book. It was filled with plenty of tips on how to proceed. This is important because you cannot just jump in.

Now, you can go out, and start working on your screenplay. This book can be your guide if you whenever get stuck.

Thank you and good luck!

OUTLINING

STEP-BY-STEP

ESSENTIAL CHAPTER OUTLINE, FICTION AND NONFICTION OUTLINING TRICKS ANY WRITER CAN LEARN

SANDY MARSH

BOOK 3: OUTLINING

STEP-BY-STEP

Essential Chapter Outline, Fiction and Nonfiction Outlining Tricks Any Writer Can Learn

Sandy Marsh

reparation, damages, or monetary loss due to the information
herein, either directly or indirectly.

Respective authors own all copyrights not held by the
publisher.

The information herein is offered for informational purposes
solely, and is universal as so. The presentation of the information
is without contract or any type of guarantee assurance.

The trademarks that are used are without any consent, and
the publication of the trademark is without permission or backing
by the trademark owner. All trademarks and brands within this
book are for clarifying purposes only and are the owned by the
owners themselves, not affiliated with this document.

Table of Contents

Introduction

Congratulations on purchasing this book and thank you for doing so. The following chapters will teach you all the important things that you need to know about making an outline. Learning to make an effective outline is an invaluable tool as a writer. It can help the writing of your book to flow more smoothly, work out more conveniently and be organized.

Chapter 1 talks about the basics of making an outline. This will give you a good foundation and understanding of what outlining is all about. Chapter 2 discusses how you can make an outline for a fiction book. Chapter 3 teaches how you can make an outline for a non-fiction book. Chapter 4 lays down the best practices that you should observe when making an outline.

Writing a book can be a daunting task. By using an outline, you can make the process of writing a book simpler and easier. The good news is that it is not hard to make an outline as long as you know what you are doing. An outline is an effective tool and is the secret behind an effective book writing. By learning how to make an outline, you are able to cover a significant part of the actual book-making process. Take the outline as a blueprint, the guide, or architecture, of your book.

Chapter 1: The Basics of Making an Outline

What is an outline?

An outline works as a guide when it comes to writing your book. Take note that a book is a big world. Without a good outline, you can easily get lost in the process of writing your book. An outline ensures that you stay within the plot that you want for your book and that every scene works towards building your story.

It is worth noting that an outline only serves as a guide. A writer has the option whether or not to stick to their outline. Still, having an outline is helpful because it will give you a sense of direction. It is also a useful tool to use to ensure proper sequencing of events or scenes in your book.

There are different ways to make an outline. This book will teach you notable and effective methods to outline a book, both for a fiction book and a non-fiction book. Indeed, learning how to make an outline is an invaluable tool that should be in the arsenal of every writer.

It can be said that an outline is the book itself but in a very simplified version. It can also deal with the technical aspects of the book, such as the timing as to when and how a certain characters or ideas will be presented. Consider the outline as the blueprint or the foundational architecture of your book.

Who uses an outline?

Almost all professional writers use an outline. Some go as far as saying that all writers *should* use an outline. The use of an outline does not just refer to books, but even in other forms of writing. In fact, it is not uncommon even for article writers to write an outline for their more complicated articles. An outline ensures that the focus of your writing and the proper flow remain concentrated. So, if making an outline is really this important, are there known authors who apply them? The answer is yes. Here are some examples to name a few: The author of *Harry Potter*, JK Rowling, James Salter, Paulo Coelho, Sylvia Plath, Jennifer

Egan, William Faulkner, and many other popular writers have admitted the use of outlines in the creation of their works. As you can see, using an outline is considered such an essential skill and tool of a writer that even well-known authors use it regularly.

Should you use an outline? Well, just because you are a writer does not necessarily mean that you are required to make an outline before writing your book. So, whether you want to use an outline or not is a matter of personal preference. Still, it is worth noting that many writers have realized the benefits of using an outline.

The importance of using an outline

It is worth noting that there are some authors who do not use an outline when they write a book. Instead, they simply allow the natural current of the work to drive them to somewhere, hoping that it would be worth telling. However, the truth is that many of these of authors have outlined the book in their mind, so somehow, they still have that sense of direction. Of course, there are also those writers who completely have no idea of what they are writing and just see where the writing goes. After all, when it comes to writing, especially when it comes to writing fiction, there are no hard and fast rules to limit a writer. You are free to write your book in whatever way you want just as you are also free not to write a book. However, if you want to be sure of your sense of direction and not waste your time writing on so many pages only to realize that they do not make sense, then you should use an outline. An outline is also easy to make, yet it will assure you that your book has a good flow and direction.

Now, there are those who say that using an outline will only limit your imagination, so they do not want to use an outline when they write a book. They do not want the outline to "cage" the expression and flow of their ideas. However, this is not the correct way to view an outline. Take note that as a writer, an outline is still just an outline. You are not in any way compelled to follow your outline all of the time. For example, let us say while you are writing the setting of the story as stated in your outline you realize that a different place would be more suitable, then you are free to use that place instead of what is in your outline. Of course, the same principle applies to the other parts of the book.

Again, an outline is a helpful guide that will ensure to give you a sense of direction; it should not, in any way, be seen as an obstacle or a cage that limits your imagination. You are strongly encouraged to stretch and explore the beauty of your mind. In fact, even an outline comes from the creative mind of a writer. The outline can be thought of as the skeleton of the book that you hang the actual story on.

Outlining for fiction vs. Non-fiction

Outlining works for any kind of book, whether fiction or non-fiction. However, making an outline for a fiction book is not the same when you make an outline for a nonfiction book and vice versa. This is because of the inherent differences between the two genres. In a fiction book, for example, a novel, you will need to spend more time outlining the plot of the story and the sequencing of the events.

You should be able to present your characters effectively and build up the story. In the case of a non-fiction book, there is usually no need to build up any story. Instead, you should focus on presenting the right information. Of course, the proper sequence should also be observed. In a fiction book, the outline will be mostly composed of the setting, the characters, and the different events that take place in the story. In a non-fiction book, the outline will be divided into main topics and subtopics regarding technical subjects.

Although there are differences between making an outline for fiction and nonfiction, the use and purpose of an outline still remain the same, and that is to make writing the book easier and more organized.

Plot outline vs. synopsis

Many people use these two terms interchangeably. However, it is worth noting that they are not the same. Take note that when you create a plot outline before even start writing a book you then use the outline as your guide as you write, so that you will be guided on how the story should flow. Writers who use plot outlines are usually called "plotters" since they plot the whole story before they even write it down. This is a good way to avoid writing too many drafts with rejected scenes and pages.

A synopsis is usually written after the completion of the book. It refers to the summary of your story or novel. The synopsis is usually a part of a proposal letter that a writer sends to a potential publisher.

A synopsis can be as short as a single page or even up to five pages. A plot outline can also take a single page but can be longer than five pages. It depends on how much you work on your outline. If you add in more details, then it will be able to guide you once you proceed to write your story. In addition to the story, a plot outline can include a detailed character story and other events.

Some writers already know their story before they even write it. So, if you can come up with the synopsis first, then you can use that as a guide to make a more detailed outline.

Understand the plot of a story

If you are into fiction writing, then it is important for you to know the plot of a story. What is a plot? It is what draws readers into the story. It refers to the arrangement of the story elements. There are generally five parts of a plot: the beginning or exposition, rising action, climax, falling action, and denouement or ending. Let us take a look at them one by one.

Exposition

The exposition is the beginning of a story. Hence, this is the part where you present your characters. Take note that the characters are not the only ones that develop your story. You also need to pay attention to the place, as well as the time. Unfortunately, some people forget about the element of time. Do not forget that Paris today was much different a hundred years ago. It is also important to keep the exposition as interesting as possible. You need to make it grab the interest of your readers; otherwise, they might stop reading your book before they even find out the about good and exciting parts.

Rising action

This is where you build up your story. This is usually where a problem is presented, and the characters take steps to face or solve the problem. This is also what prepares the most exciting part of the story, the climax. The rising action is where you build up the anxiety and the expectations. This is also the part where you start to tug at the hearts and emotions of your readers. The more attached the readers are to the characters, the more powerful the climax and the overall story will be. It is important that a writer build up the story effectively; otherwise, the story may become boring to the reader.

Climax

This is known as the turning point and the most exciting part of the story. This is where the emotions are at their peak. Nothing is ever the same as this point. This is where real and solid changes take place. Usually, immediately right after the climax, everything takes a downhill, relaxes, and prepares for the ending.

Falling action

This is the part where the story falls and takes a downhill, which leads to the ending of the story. Here, the story usually comes together, and the missing pieces are finally resolved. This is also where you reward your audience. Take note that your readers normally associate themselves with the protagonist in the story, so you use this part show them how the protagonist is rewarded for all of his or her labor. This is also a good part to impress on the readers the moral of your story if any.

Denouement

This is the ending of the story. Here, the loose ends are tied, and the questions are finally answered. Of course, it can be a happy ending or a sad ending. A story can even have an open ending where there is technically no end and you leave to the reader the final conclusion of the story.

Why is it important to understand the plot?

As a writer, it is important for you to understand the plot. When you make an outline, you actually work on the plot of your story, such as how are you going to begin the story, how do you present your characters, the time and place, etc. before then you moving on to the rising action, then the climax, and so on. As you can see, it is important to have a good understanding of the plot because the story revolves around the plot that you set. There are also writers who make an outline by simply filling in the parts of the plot with details.

Chapter 2: Fiction Outline

Snowball Method

The snowball method is one of the most popular techniques for making an outline. Just like a rolling snowball that gets bigger and bigger as it rolls downhill, the snowball method starts with just a simple topic, idea, or a scene. It will then be continuously developed, and it will branch out to more ideas, more scenes, and other parts of the story.

For example, let's start with the simple idea of a man who falls in love with a woman. Let this idea be the very center of the snowball. This will also be the main theme of the story. We now branch out a little and give them each a name. Let us say that the name of the man is Jack and the name of the woman is Mina. So now we have the protagonists of the story, as well as the central theme of love. Of course, Jack cannot just fall in love with Mina out of nowhere. So, we add another part to our snowball: let us say for example that Mina is in need of money. She then applies for a job at a nearby restaurant which happens to be owned by Jack. Let us say that Mina is able to get the job as a waitress, and she then works as a waitress gets to meet other people who work at the restaurant. Again, this is another part of the snowball.

When working as a waitress, one day, Mina encounters a very rude customer. Again, we let the snowball turn, and we simply continue to add more information or details. For example, let us say that the rude customer is the one who complains and calls for the manager of the restaurant who happens to be Jack as well, the owner. Jack then is able to put the situation under control. That evening, Jack calls Mina to his office for a meeting. Mina is anxious about it because she does not want to lose her job. Again, we simply let the snowball turn and gather more details. Contrary to what she has expected, once she is already in the office, Jack appears to be very polite and even apologizes for what happened that day.

This is simply how the snowball method works. Simply put, you just have to keep adding more and more details. If you continue to do this, then you will soon come up with a short story, a novelette, or even a novel. From one small snowball, you simply let it roll and roll and gather more ideas and details to turn it into a big snowball, a complete story. Also, do not forget that you are writing an outline and not a story just yet. So, keep it simple and short, but be sure that the main points of the story are there.

Pure summary

As the name implies, a pure summary outline is the kind of outline that is composed of summaries. This is like the short version of your entire book or novel. You simply have to summarize everything, such as chapters, scenes, and others.

The idea behind this method is to write down your whole story from beginning to end, but only write down a compressed version. To do this, just write down the important parts or highlights. You can skip all forms of dialogues and just focus on telling what is happening in the story.

For example, Ana is looking for a job and applies as a journalist. She gets the job and as she works as a journalist, she gets to meet Ryan, a photographer, who happens to work in the same company. Despite their busy schedule, they do their best to make time for each other. One day, Ana is in an accident and

Ryan does his best to serve her. To save her life, he has to go into an ancient forest and get a golden apple from a mysterious tree. He ventures into the forest and meets Galdorf, a friendly elf. Galdorf helps him find the mysterious tree and battle the Dark Witch of the forest. By doing so, he frees the imprisoned elves and also saves Ana from dying. They live happily ever after.

As you can see, every part of the story is compressed but it is complete. All that you need to do is to fill in the details. The good thing here is that you are already given a clear roadmap or guideline as to how your story will flow from start to finish. In fact, by using this approach, you will already be able to imagine your story as a whole, and all that you need to do is to write down the details to make the story come alive.

The pure summary is one of the best ways to make an outline. Just summarize every chapter or sub-chapter from beginning to end. When done, you will have a complete story. All that you need to do is to clarify every point by adding in more details.

Skeletal outline

You have probably learned this kind of outline in school or for any other academic purposes. The key to this method is to input the core points in the right order that will best present your story. This is an effective way to get a bird's eye view of your story, including its overall structure. Take note that the structure of a book or story is essential. A book that is poorly structured, whether fiction or non-fiction, will most probably have problems with being disorganized and have confusing contents. A skeletal outline will allow you to easily reform your story or book, which will allow you to create the maximum impact out of your story. Let us take a look at a simple example of a skeletal outline:

Exposition

- The setting of the story takes place in a small village called as Sestin.

- The story introduces Adam, who is a farmer.

- The story then introduces Monica, the daughter of a rich businessman

Rising action

- Adam meets Monica as he tends the farm of her father.

- They get to know each other for some days.

- One day, goblins attack the village of Sestin.

- Monica is held hostage by the goblins.

Climax

- Adam fights the goblins and saves Monica.

- The story also reveals that they both share the same mutual feeling for each other.

- It is found that Adam is actually of royal blood and owns a kingdom

Falling action

- The father of Monica allows Adam to marry his daughter

Denouement

- Adam and Monica get married and everyone is happy.

- They all live happily ever after.

Take note that this is just an example of a skeletal outline. It may be shorter or even much longer than this. The important thing is to plot the story and the events properly. It is also worth noting that this kind of outline is not just applicable to fiction writing. You can also use it for non-fiction works. This will be discussed in more detail later in the book.

A good thing about this approach is that it allows you to see the structure of your book more clearly. Usually, a skeletal outline clearly divides the book into parts and is just composed of single lines. When taken together, they all compose a whole story.

Bullet outline

- A bullet outline is one of the most common types of outlining. In fact, this is one that is widely used by people even if they do not read about it. With a bullet outline, you simply have to make notes in bullet form as to what will happen in the story. For example:

- Lisa is an accountant.

- One day, she meets Mr. Gibson, a high-stakes gambler.

- They get to know each other better.

- They fall in love with each other.

- However, Mr. Gibson's gambling addiction starts to become a problem and begins to affect their relationship.

- Lisa tries to help Mr. Gibson and does her best to save their relationship.

- (and so on and so forth)

This is an example of a bullet outline. So, how do you use this outline? It is actually fairly simple. Using the example, at first you expound on the part of the outline that says, "Lisa is an accountant." A good way to do this when you actually write your novel is to describe the nature of Lisa's work. Make it as meaningful and interesting as possible.

If you look at the next part of the sample outline, the next part is "One day, she meets Mr. Gibson, a high-stakes gambler." Of course, you would not have to write this line as is. Rather, just like the first bullet, you make it more details. How did they meet? Perhaps Mr. Gibson starts to have money problems and needs an accountant to save his business. You can explore and expound on this once you actually start to write the book. Take note that this single bullet alone can take a whole chapter. This is just to give you an example of how to use a bullet outline more effectively.

A bullet outline is a very simple yet effective method. Another benefit of using this kind of outline is that it gives you a lot of room to exercise your imagination once you start to write the story. The outline focuses more on the flow of the story instead of what is actually happening in the story.

It is common to use a bullet outline on a per chapter basis. Many writers first prepare an outline in bullet form before they begin writing a chapter. This way, they can be sure that they know the direction of the story. Every bullet point is also usually short, so it would not be hard for you to follow it. Once you have a well-established outline in bullet form, then all you need to do is fill in the details of every bullet point and not worry about the direction that your story will take.

Chapter outline

A chapter outline divides a story into chapters. Every chapter will then have an outline of what is going to happen in that particular chapter. Here is an example:

Chapter 1: The Meeting

Noah calls for all the soldiers to attend the secret meeting.

Every soldier attends the meeting, except for Jason.

Jason, the number one soldier in the world, wakes up in a hospital with amnesia.

Even though Jason is not able to attend the meeting set by Noah, Noah is soon able to follow his tracks and visits him in the hospital.

Noah reminds Jason who he really is.

As you can see from the example, the book will be divided into chapters and every chapter will then be divided into sub-topics or events that take place in the story. A chapter outline is a good method, especially if you are particular with every chapter in your book.

As is usual, only the main points are included. This is to give room for you to exercise your creative imagination when you write the story. The outline is just enough to guide you as to what will happen next and avoid the situation where you get stuck up not knowing how to make the story to flow continuously. A chapter outline is also one that is commonly used by writers.

Sequence outline

A sequence outline puts more focus upon the sequencing of the events in the story. However, it still outlines the important points, so even this method alone would be enough to help you with writing your book. Here is an example of this kind of outline:

1 - Dianne, still a very young child, is baptized as a witch.

2 - Her parents were killed for practicing sorcery.

3 - She soon grows into one of the most powerful witches.

4 - Dianne meets King Gregory, the man who had ordered for her parents to be burned at the stake.

(and so on and so forth)

As you can see, there is a fine outline of the sequence of the events. If you are the type of writer who finds it hard to stick to the flow of your story, then a sequence outline may be the one for you.

Although you can add in as many details as you want, it is important to stick to the sequence; otherwise, a change may have major effects on the story as a whole. Take note that if you mess up with even just one part of the sequence, then you should check how it affects the other parts. Are they still logical enough when taken together? This method is also commonly used by writers. It is also like a bullet form outline but is more particular with the sequence of the events and the flow of the story.

Flowchart outline

This approach makes use of a flowchart. This is similar to a sequence outline but makes use of a chart that is also in proper sequence. Here is a simple example:

Adam works as a painter --> He attends an event for artists -> While at the event, he sees and meets Stella --> He falls in love with her at first sight --> and so on and so forth.

As you can see, the scenes or parts of the chapters are reflected through this flowchart. When you finally start working on the book, then you will add in the details to every point in the chart. A single part of the flowchart can cover a few pages up to a whole chapter, depending on what is happening in your story. So, for example, let us take the first part of the flowchart: Adam works as a painter. When you write this in your book, you can then expound on this topic. You describe the nature of his work and you can also write and show what happens in his life as a painter. As you can see, just these things alone can take many pages, even a whole chapter.

The thing with a flowchart method, just like any other outlining method, is for you to pinpoint the main parts of the story and ensure that you arrange things in the right order. Once everything is set, then you simply have to add the details when you write the book.

Visual outline

If you are fond of drawing, then this style of outlining may be the one for you. When you use a visual outline, all that you need to do is to draw the main events in a story, especially its plot. Take note that instead of writing in words, this approach lies in drawing and making figures. For this, you may want to use a notebook. You can fill each page with a drawing that would illustrate what the scene will be. You then follow it up with another scene on the next page, and so on and so forth.

Even if you cannot draw well, you can still use this approach. After all, just like any other outlines, this is something that you do not need to show to anyone else. An advantage of using drawings instead of words in making an outline is that you will have more room to play with the words, as well as for the exercise of your imagination. This is because every drawing can have diverse meanings and significance. If you want a style of outline that will give you maximum use of your imagination once you begin writing your book, then perhaps using a visual outline is a good idea. However, the drawback is that this kind of outlining may not always work for everyone. In fact, the very reason why you want to make an outline is to have a good sense of direction when you finally write your book. The risk is that you may not be so inspired when you finally write your book that the drawings may start to look boring or empty to you.

Chapter 3: Non-Fiction Outline

Pure summary

Just like for fiction writing, you can also use the pure summary approach for non-fiction book writing. When you use this approach, simply make a summary of the information. This means that you do not have to explain anything. Just make a summary of every chapter in the book. For sub-topics, you can simply write a one or two-sentence summary. Again, this is just a summary, so there is no need for you to expound or explain anything. Still, it is worth noting that when you read a summary, the stories must be coherent and logical enough. In other words, it must still be a complete story with proper flow and structure. However, of course, you do not want for it to too detailed. After all, it is just a summary, which can be a summary per chapter or even per sub-topic in every chapter. The important thing is for the summary to mention the main points of the book. This will also ensure that you will not forget about them.

When you use this method, then it is also important that you pay attention to the sequence of the information. A common rule in non-fiction writing is to start from the basics, and then gradually branch out to more complicated matters on the subject.

In non-fiction, you are not expected to make a well-detailed summary considering that there is a chance that you still need to learn more specific details about the topic in question. Of course, if you know exactly what you are writing about then you may only require a minimum level of research; however, if you are writing something about which you do not have enough knowledge, then there would be little that needs to be summarized. If you want, you can just research and study the subject first before you start to make a pure summary outline. However, do not let the lack of research prevent you from using this approach. After all, you have the convenience of having open books and information both when you make an outline and when you write the book.

Skeletal outline

A skeletal outline is common in non-fiction writing, especially when the book deals with a technical topic. This is because a skeletal outline offers exactly what you would need for non-fiction writing. When you use this approach, you begin with a subtitle, which may be the name of your chapter. You then identify and specify the skeletal outline of the book with the topics and sub-topics that you will discuss in the book. Needless to say, this follows the same format as the one for fiction. However, unlike a fiction book, this does not follow any plot. Rather, it has a more logical flow to it. For example, when you write a book about bitcoin, you should not talk about bitcoin mining right away. Instead, you should start with the basics, such as what bitcoin is, what a cryptocurrency is, and others, and then make your way up from there.

Bullet outline

A bullet outline is excellent when you deal with specifics. For example, when you make an outline of a chapter or sub-chapter in a book. Also, what you can do is to highlight the name of a chapter, and then simply outline in bullet form what you want to talk about for that part of the book. For example, let us say that you want to write a book about the cryptocurrency Bitcoin, here is a sample outline:

Chapter 1: The Basics of Bitcoin

- What is Bitcoin?

- What is cryptocurrency?

- What is a cryptocurrency wallet?

- Who uses bitcoin

- How does a bitcoin transaction work?

- (and others)

As you can see, every point is made clear. All that is left for you to do is add the details. Of course, you can further use the bullet outline like this:

Chapter 1: The Basics of Bitcoin

- What is Bitcoin?

    - a digital money

    - uses cryptography

- What is cryptocurrency?

    - cryptography for secure communication and transaction

- What is a cryptocurrency wallet?

    - a place to store cryptocurrency

    - kinds of cryptocurrency wallets (hot and cold wallets)

- Who uses bitcoin

- anyone with an Internet connection

- How does a bitcoin transaction work?

  - Input

  - Recipient's wallet address

  - Amount

As you can see, this makes it more detailed and it will be easier to fill in the information once you start writing the book. When you write non-fiction, outlining your work is more practical. After all, non-fiction works do not deal so much with one's creative imagination. The important thing is for you to be able to cover the technical details and be able to present them effectively.

Chapter outline

A chapter outline is one of the simplest ways to make an outline for a non-fiction book. Basically, you simply have to write the name of the chapter, and then add in the titles of the sub-topics within a chapter. This is also like a bullet form of outlining but is more general. Of course, you can also make it more specific by further outlining the sub-topics just like in a bullet outline. In fact, both kinds of outline are very similar to each other.

The first step in a chapter outline is to set the titles of the chapters. Again, as a rule in non-fiction, you should start with the basics. The reason is that you must first establish a foundation for your readers before you delve into more complicated matters. A common mistake committed by writers is to assume that the reader already knows and understands the topic. If you come to think of it, this understanding is highly flawed. After all, a reader would not have to waste time reading your book if he is already aware or if he already understands what is written in your book. So, never assume that the reader can easily understand what you write. Instead, have an open mind and consider the reader as someone who knows nothing about your subject. Of course, this is subject to some exceptions, for example, if you target readers are really those who already have an idea of your subject. A good example of this will be the advanced guides or manuals.

Once you have the titles of the different chapter ready, then it is time for you to add in the subtitles that will be placed under each corresponding chapter. You should be careful about the subtitles because they are the ones that will lead the development of the book. Hence, they are the ones that will form the structure of the book. Just stick to the basic rule of starting with the basics and then work your way up, and you will be fine. This is just a matter of presentation. Feel free to try different combinations until you find the one that feels most natural and convenient for a reader.

The number of chapters will depend on the kind of book that you write, as well as the number of words of the entire book. Normally, the longer the book is, the more chapters it will include. When you write your outline, be sure to pay attention to how many chapters your book will have, as well as the number of sub-topics that you will be using. It helps if you have more sub-topics so that you will not run out of things to write about. However, take note that book writing is not about the length but the quality if your book. Hence, it is important that you focus more on the quality of your writing that on the number of chapters or subtitles that your book has.

Research

Although not considered as a complete outlining method, when it comes to non-fiction writing, research is the main tool that you have in your arsenal. Although you are still free to use your imagination, non-fiction writing has certain restraints upon one's writing. The golden rule is that you cannot contradict a fact. Well, except, of course, if you have another set of facts to present that can support your view. Take note that when it comes to non-fiction writing, the facts are your friends. Needless to say, in a non-fiction book, almost everything that you write should be backed up by research or at least verifiable. This is to make your writing more believable and credible.

In non-fiction writing, it does not matter how good your outline is if you do not understand the subject. Hence, make sure that you have all the necessary materials to get to know your subject and do as much research as possible. The more that you know your subject, the easier it will be for you to come up with a good outline, and the easier it will be for you to complete the book.

Chapter 4: Best Practices

Know your characters

When you write a story, especially in fiction writing, it is important for you to know your characters. It is worth noting that an outline is not something that you use to get to know your characters. It is important for you to know the characters first before you make an outline.

Take note that the characters are important as they are the ones that tell and develop the story. If there are not enough characters or if you do not know your characters well enough, then the story will not grow properly. Therefore, is important for you to know and understand who your characters are. In fact, once you know your characters, then telling the story will come naturally as the characters themselves will play out the story. This is the part of writing a story where the writer becomes a mere observer of his characters. You can allow your characters to lead you. This will give you an idea of what the story will be and, so it will be easier for you to make an outline.

If you do not know your characters yet, especially your main characters in the story, then you should give yourself more time to get to know them. You do not necessarily have to know all your characters completely. You will know if you already have sufficient understanding of your characters when the characters themselves are able to lead and create the story for you. Needless to say, every character must have his or her own persona and should act according to that personality.

A suggested way to know your characters is to interview them one by one. This is a common practice used by novel writers. So, how does it work? Just imagine talking to your character. Ask them questions and see and feel how they respond. This may seem strange to some people, but many writers use this approach. They talk to their characters to the point like they feel that they are merely recording (writing) what the characters in the story are telling them. Once characters are given a persona and existence in the story, it will seem that they really have an identity and life of their own. Hence, talk with your characters and ask them questions. Learn from them. This way you will be more able to develop your story.

Know your story

Take note that your plot is like the skeleton of your story. Therefore, when you write a plot it is also important that you already have an idea of what your story is going to be. When you write an outline, it is not important for you to know the minor details and the dialogues of the characters. However, it is important for you to know the main points of your story or the main events that will shape your story. These are the things that will constitute your outline.

The more that you know your story, the easier it will be for you to make an outline of it. After all, making an outline is as simple as recording essential details and skipping dialogues and other things that are considered important to a novel. It is more focused on simply having a worthwhile story instead of discussing all the things that happen in a story.

Now, it is also worth noting that many writers write an outline even without knowing their story. How is this possible? Well, they allow the process of outlining to reveal the story to them. To do this, you just need a basic idea. You write it down as part of an outline, and then simply add more details to it to continue to grow your idea. Since you are just making an outline, it does not have to be too detailed, and you should just focus on the main points that will help develop the story.

Keep it simple

It is important to keep your outline simple. Remember that your outline should not be a cage that will limit your imagination. Rather, it should serve as a guide that will help you come up with a meaningful story. Therefore, keep your outline simple, including only the main and important points that should be in your story.

As a rule, small or minor details should not be placed in an outline, except if they are important to the story. The reason why you do not include everything in your outline is to prevent the outline from limiting you to exercise your imagination as you write your story. Again, an outline should only serve as a guide.

You also do not have to make your outline beautifully worded. Do not forget that the outline is only for your own eyes, so you do not have to spend so much effort in finding the right combination of words. You can save such effort for when you finally write the book. Instead of worrying about the words that you use, focus on the story that you want to tell, as well as the flow of the events and information.

Be flexible

It is worth remembering that an outline only functions as a guide. As such, it is not required for you to always stick to your outline. This is important for you to remember, especially if you suddenly come up with a better idea than the one in your outline while writing the story. This is another reason why you should keep your outline as simple as possible. By keeping it simple and just including the important parts of the story, then you will have more room to exercise your imagination.

It is considered very common for writers to suddenly stray away from their original outline. This is why you should not spend so much time worrying about how your outline is written. After all, it is still just a guide for you; and being the writer, you are free not to follow your outline.

Flexibility is important. Normally, the story only reveals itself fully even to the writer only when you actually pen down the story. This may sometimes come as a surprise, even to the author himself. As you write your book, the more you realize what the story is really all about. Simply put, as you follow your outline, you are also led to discover more about it. Now, from time to time, you may have to change course and take a completely different one than what you have originally outlined. This is normal, but just be sure to take a better path than the previous or current one. Also, if you ever change your course, you may want to stop for a while and reflect on the direction of your new outline.

A normal part of flexibility is to be flexible enough to update your outline. Yes, an outline can undergo so many changes and modifications as you write your book. Take note that you do not need to write new outlines, rather you can just edit your current outline little by little.

A common mistake committed by writers is to change a part in an outline and then allow the new storyline to lead the way without him knowing where it will actually go. Then this happens, then it is as good as writing without an outline. Now, I am not saying that this approach is wrong. Again, there are no hard and fast rules about how to write a book. However, if you are the type who cannot write properly and organize your thoughts without a guide, then what you should do in this case is to update your outline. Yes, updating an outline is something that you should do every time you make even minor changes to your outline. The outline must remain logical and coherent all throughout. This will ensure that your novel or the story itself will also be logical, coherent, and well structured. After all, your very story is just the outline itself, only that it now has more details. For example, if your outline says that Samantha is beautiful, then your story will make descriptions or show certain scenes to show just how beautiful she is. Still, the very essence of the writing can be traced back to your simple outline. Outlining and being flexible go hand in hand. Although there are writers who stick completely to their original outline and do not let anything divert their path (which is not wrong per se), sometimes it is good to be more open and allow changes to take place, especially positive changes.

Have a clear premise

Even before you work on an outline, you should first establish your premise. Ask yourself:

- Who is/are my main character/s in the story?

- Where does the story take place? In what year or time?

- What is the conflict in the story?

- What will be the turning point of my story?

- What message do I want the story to communicate to the readers?

- Who will be the enemies in the story, if any?

Once you have answered all these questions, then it means that you have a good idea of what your story will be. Take note that these are just basic questions. You are free to expound and ask more specific questions. But, these questions will reveal to you the premise of your story or what it is really about. Now, in case you find it hard to answer these simple questions, then it only means that you need to think about your story even more. Do not forget that an outline can only be made if you have a story to tell. Although an outline does not need a complete story, it requires that its essential elements should be present.

When you ask yourself these questions, it is important that you be completely honest with yourself. It is unfortunate that some writers delude themselves and hate saying" I don't know." Take note that this is a normal part of the writing process. The more that you admit to yourself the parts in your story that are still unclear to you, then the more you will understand what your story is really about. After all, the act of writing is still an act of self-discovery. You do not need to have the answers right away. It is normal to accept that you do not know the answers to some questions; the important thing is not to stop to seek for an answer. Of course, to do this, you need to reflect and delve more into your story.

Take a break

Just as you take some breaks to finish writing a book, you should also give yourself time to take a break when you are working on an outline. It is not uncommon for professional writers to spends days just to work on their outline. If you are just starting out to learn how to write and use an outline, then feel free to take as much time as you need. Just do not forget that an outline should make the writing of the book to easier in the long run. Unfortunately, some writers get too caught up writing their outlines that they fail to even start writing the actual book.

You will also be able to think much more clearly and be more creative if you allow your mind to relax. In fact, writers are strongly advised to give themselves a break from time to time even while working on the actual book. It is not uncommon to find writers who go to the beach and spend time on vacation while working on a book. This is because you will be a much more effective writer when you allow yourself to rest. With a fresh and rejuvenated mind, you will be able to use your creative talent more effectively.

Choose and organize your ideas

A book comes from an outline. But, where does an outline come from? Yes – an outline comes from ideas. However, it is worth noting that in the process of writing a book, it is very common to experience being bombarded with lots of ideas. For example, let us take a simple example where you present a protagonist in a story. Let us say that your hero is a man who happens to work in secret service for the government. There are tons of different ideas that you can use to show this. There are also many ways by which the story can go. Does he have super powers? Is he going to die and then resurrect? Or is he just an ordinary person who just happens to be good at what he does or maybe he is not even good at his job and merely relies on luck. The thing is that although outlining is a way to record and organize your ideas, you should also choose the ideas that you will be using in your story.

Now, once you have organized the ideas in your mind, it will then be easy for you to plot your story by making an outline. It is simply hard to make an outline when you know that you yourself do not know your story.

Observe proper sequence

When you write your way outline, it is important for you to pay attention to the proper sequence of the events or information. If it is a fiction book, I then the building and arrangement of the story should be in proper order. If you are writing a non-fiction book, then the information should be in an ordered sequence that will make the information more understandable to your audience. This is important especially if you are writing about a technical topic. For a fiction book, you should build up the story from beginning up to the end. In case of a non-fiction book, then you should share the information by starting from the basic details, and then continue building your way up to more complicated topics or sub-topics in the book.

Making an outline is the best way to set the proper sequencing of events of your story. Unfortunately, some writers still write the bulk of words only to end up with a confusing storyline. By making an outline, you can easily work on the sequence of the events of your story. In fact, you will be able to view and imagine your story completely, and all that will be left for you to do is to add in the details.

If you ever find yourself having a hard time putting things in the right sequence of ideas or events, then it is usually a sign that you should pause for a while and try to understand what is really going on in your story. Sometimes the logical sequence itself will be the one to guide you as to what to write next.

Focus on the main points

Making an outline is simply making a list of the important points of the book in proper order. You should focus on the main points. For a fiction book, the main points will be the beginning of the story, the rising action, climax, falling action, and the denouement. In the case of a non-fiction book, the main points, of course, would relate to the important details regarding your subject.

It is worth noting that some minor details may also be considered a necessary element in the development of a story. In this case, you can include the said minor details in your outline.

But, what are the main points? How do you know if a certain detail should be considered a main point and be included in your outline or not? Well, it depends. If the detail or information is something that is important in building up the story, then it is to be considered a main point and should be included in your outline. However, if it is something that your book or story can do without, then it is just a minor detail. The important thing about making an outline is to give you a good sense of direction. It has to function as a logical road map of your thoughts even if you forget about your story. After all, it is not uncommon for writers to think of an exciting plot only to have it slip away before they are able to get it written down completely. Whenever this happens, a possible wonderful story is lost to the world.

It does not have to be perfect

An outline does not need to be perfect. Keep in mind that it is just a guide. Hence, there is no need to follow it to the letter. Even if you come up with what you believe to be a perfect outline, know that it is still just an outline. As such, you should not allow yourself to be limited by it.

It is also worth noting that no matter how perfect you think your outline is, there is still a chance that it may be revised or modified. This is true, especially in the case of novels. It is not uncommon for writers to start at something specific only to be taken by the story somewhere more beautiful than they had imagined before writing the book. Does this mean that writing an outline is not important? Of course not. An outline assures that you maintain sense and direction in your story. However, it is worth noting that it considered common for writers to make changes to their outline several times as they write the book. Now, you should be careful when you do this. As a general rule, you should not change your original outline. You must stick to it. However, as an exception, you may change your outline if you are able to come up with a better version of the story. It has to make the story more exciting or meaningful for the readers. If not, then you need to stick to your outline. This is the reason why you should not aim to have a perfect outline because such a thing simply does not exist.

Although you do not expect an outline to be perfect, it does not mean that the outline can just contain every thought that you think would be good for your story. An outline must still be carefully written. How can you expect for your outline to guide you if the ideas do not match up well with one another or if the outline itself fails to follow a logical sequence? Hence, it is important that you work on your outline, but do not aim for perfection. Having the right ideas and correct flow would be enough.

Now, just because an outline does not have to be perfect does not mean that you should not give it as much time as it deserves. The outline, after all, serves as the foundation of your book. Therefore, take as much time as you need when making your outline, which leads us to the next topic: time.

Remember that an outline is just a guide

Although an outline can be regarded as important, do not forget the fact that an outline is still just your guide. Therefore, you are free to stick to it while you write the book or totally abandon it halfway. However, this does not mean that an outline is no longer important. But, you need to understand this so that you will not end up like other writers who get too obsessed with their outline.

Remember to see and use your outline as a guide in writing the book. You are always free to change or revise your outline as many times as you want and in any way that you deem best.

Take your time

When making an outline, you should take as much time as you need. Although your outline will not be a part of your book, it is still the foundation of your book. Consider it like a business plan or blueprint of your masterpiece.

Although you can make an outline in as fast as a few minutes, it is not uncommon for professional writers to spend even a week to work on an outline. This is true, especially if you want to create a high-quality book.

You should also learn to organize and manage your time. Unfortunately, there are many writers who commit the mistake of procrastinating. The temptation to procrastinate is something that you should watch out for when you write a book. A good way to avoid procrastination is to set daily objectives. For example, aim to be able to finish 15% of your outline every day. Also, take note that writing an outline is just part of the process. The more important part is for you to write your book, which will take more time and effort than writing an outline.

Have your sources ready

This is true, especially if you work on a non-fiction book. You should have your sources ready. This is because sometimes it is hard to look for your sources during the time of actual writing. A good way to keep your outline more organized is to cite your sources in the outline. One of the main reasons for using an outline is to make the work of writing the book easier for you.

You do not have to cite your sources formally. After all, the outline is your own private document. You do not need to show it to your readers or anyone else. The purpose of having your sources ready and to cite your sources is for you to be ready when you write your book. So that when you write the book, you will know exactly where to look for information as you fill in every major and minor topic in your outline. Even fiction writers can use the same approach. After all, many fiction stories also incorporate real-life events. Take, for example, *Da Vinci Code*, which combines fiction with non-fiction information.

When it comes to writing non-fiction, it is important to take note that you should stick to the facts. If you want to force your creative thought and ideas into the page, then you might want to consider shifting to fiction writing. It is worth noting that readers of non-fiction books read not mainly for entertainment or pleasure, but to get as much as useful information as possible. They do not care about your opinions unless your views have a good basis and foundation. Hence, it is important to identify the kind of genre that you want to write in even before you make an outline. This is because the style of writing and even the expectation of the readers have certain distinctions between fiction and non-fiction writing. As for the sources, be sure to quote from credible sources. If possible, use internationally known and accepted formats like APA or Chicago when citing your sources.

Ask yourself questions

Okay, so now you have a clear idea of how to make an outline. But, how do you know which types to include in your outline? The key is to ask yourself questions, the right questions. For example, when writing fiction, let us say that you have a character named Max. Now, ask yourself, who is Max? Let us say that Max is a poet.

Ask yourself who is Max as a poet? What is he like? Once you are able to answer this then you can have something to place in your outline: Max is a poet who writes for a princess who does not even know that he loves her. Next, ask yourself what happens next. You may come up with the next part of the outline, like: A big event is about to take place and Max and the princess are going to attend the said event. The next step is for you to imagine the event and ask yourself what happens to Max at the event, and so on and so forth. As you can see, by simply asking yourself the right questions, you can develop a story.

How about for non-fiction writing? Well, a similar technique can be used. However, if you are dealing with a technical topic, let us say a book about Blockchain technology, then you should ask a different kind of questions. For example: What is blockchain? What are the types of blockchain? What is the history of blockchain? This continues until you come up with a highly informative book.

It is important to ensure that every part of your outline should help develop or enhance the book. This way you can be sure that your book will be interesting and informative.

Okay, so how do you know the right questions to ask? It is simple. You just have to take the perspective of a reader who does not know your book or subject. Therefore, if it is fiction writing or when you write a novel, if you have a character in mind named Gabriel, then ask: Who is Gabriel? What does he do? Where does he live? All these questions will soon open up a whole new story that is full of meaning and value. Now, in the case of non-fiction writing, again just consider that a reader is a beginner in the subject that you are discussing. Therefore, you should start with the basic details and lay down a good foundation. After which, you can then talk about more complicated topics within your subject matter.

Practice

When it comes to learning how to outline properly and more effectively, nothing beats practice. So, if you want to learn how to make an outline, then just start practicing it. Make an outline for the next books that you write. No matter how much you read about it, it remains true that the only way for you to appreciate and realize just how beneficial making an outline can be.

Learning how to write a good outline is just like learning to write good books. This means that you simply have to practice it by applying it regularly. If you get good at writing outlines, then the task of writing a book becomes simpler and more manageable.

You do not have to learn the different ways to outline a book. After all, when you make an outline, you only need to use one method. If you want, you can combine two methods at once. There is no strict rule as to when a particular method should be used over another. Therefore, feel free to use the one that you are most comfortable with.

For those writers who are against the use of an outline:

Indeed, there are some writers who do not like the idea of using an outline. It is worth noting that this book does not make it a requirement or an obligation of a writer to use an outline, but merely shares how helpful an outline can be in the process of writing a book. Therefore, if you strongly prefer not to use an outline, then you are free to do so. In the world of book writing, whether or not you use an outline does not matter in the end. What matters is the final product, which is the book itself. There are writers who use an outline and know for sure how useful it is, while there are those who simply allow the story to unfold like a surprise. The only disadvantage of not having an outline is that it is common to follow a story only to meet a dead end or you just realize that the story has become dull and boring.

An outline assures that before you even start working and writing your boo, you are assured of a good sense of direction. All you need to do is write, and even if all that you do is to stick to your outline and not change any parts of the story but merely add in the details pursuant to your outline, then you can be sure that you will end up with a good book, provided that you have prepared a good outline.

Once again, it is up to you as a writer whether or not to use an outline. The best way to find out what works for you would be to give it a try. Write a book without an outline and then write one that has a proper outline, and see which writing experience is better for you. In the end, it is not about whether or not you have used an outline, but how much the book has made your soul grow in the process.

Conclusion

Thanks for making it through to the end of this book. We hope it was informative and able to provide you with all of the tools you need to achieve your goals whatever they may be.

The next step is to apply everything that you have learned and start making an outline of your book. Learning how to make an outline is one of the best things that should be in the arsenal of every writer. It is useful and makes the book writing process easy and manageable.

If you are a beginner, you might encounter some difficulties writing an outline for the first time. The key is to not be too strict about it. It is worth noting that the methods revealed in this book are also just guides. You, as the writer, has all the right to make your own modifications. In fact, you may want to develop your own way of making an outline. The important thing is for you to know and understand how to use it to help you in writing a book. Keep in mind that there is really no right and wrong way of making an outline as long as it is able to help you write your book. After all, the very purpose of an outline is to help a writer and make the process of writing a book simpler, easier, and more organized.

When you write a book, it is not uncommon to suddenly feel so lost. Some writers have a story to tell but do not know how to start or how to maintain a smooth flow of the pages. This is why making an outline is important. There is a big universe out there, and you need to place only the right stuff into your book in proper order. Indeed, the task of a writer is not an easy thing. But, if you learn how to use an outline, then you have an invaluable weapon that you can use to make the writing process so much easier.

Good luck!

STORY STRUCTURE

STEP-BY-STEP

ESSENTIAL STORY BUILDING, STORY DEVELOPMENT AND SUSPENSE WRITING TRICKS ANY WRITER CAN LEARN

SANDY MARSH

BOOK 4: STORY STRUCTURE

STEP-BY-STEP

Essential Story Building, Story Development and Suspense Writing Tricks Any Writer Can Learn

Sandy Marsh

reparation, damages, or monetary loss due to the information herein, either directly or indirectly.

Respective authors own all copyrights not held by the publisher.

The information herein is offered for informational purposes solely, and is universal as so. The presentation of the information is without contract or any type of guarantee assurance.

The trademarks that are used are without any consent, and the publication of the trademark is without permission or backing by the trademark owner. All trademarks and brands within this book are for clarifying purposes only and are the owned by the owners themselves, not affiliated with this document.

Table of Contents

Introduction

Thank you and congratulations on purchasing *"Story Structure: Step-by-Step | Essential Story Building, Story Development and Suspense Writing Tricks Any Writer Can Learn"*.

This book was created to help you learn a series of tips and tricks that will help you enrich your story and make it a must-read book for your target audience. By using these techniques and strategies in your own book you will be able to generate a storyline that is rich with suspense, action, and other tools that are important to keep your readers engaged and excited about reading your book.

Each chapter within' this book is dedicated to one element of story structures themselves, ensuring that you are provided with the greatest in-depth detail to ensure that you learn plenty to help you produce a phenomenal story. Before the book ends, you will be provided with tips from top writers and authors that will help you write like the pros.

This book was not designed for any particular experience level when it comes to writing. Instead, it has been populated with tricks that will help any writer from beginner to advanced. If you are someone who typically struggles to write stories but you are looking to get yours heard, you can be certain that you will learn some tips here to help you get on your way towards having your book completed. Likewise, if you have done this before but are looking for a refresher or are otherwise interested in learning more to enrich your story and create an addictive read for your audience, you are certainly going to learn something also.

Please be sure to take your time and work through all of the tips and tricks provided within' this book. While some may not be entirely relevant to the work you are producing, they may provide you with inspiration to move forward in a more powerful way. As well, be sure to keep this book handy for future writing ventures as you never know which part will stand out each time. Finally, remember that writing is an experience that should be enjoyed by both the reader and the author. Be sure that you take the time to make the process enjoyable for yourself so that you can produce your best work. And finally, have fun!

Chapter 1: Purpose of Story Structure

Understanding the purpose of story structure will ensure that you are aware of how it can make (or break) your story, and why it is so crucial that you develop a strong structure within' your own story. Prior to diving into any important tips or strategies, we are going to explore what a story structure is, exactly, and what purpose it serves within' your story.

What is a Story Structure?

In basic form, a story structure is essentially a map that is drawn to take your reader from point a to point b. You want them to start at the beginning of the book and end at the end, only after being taken through an experience which is essentially each "stop" on the map. This map is used to help identify how people solve different problems, as well as to assist in conveying the message that the author is attempting to send from the storytelling process. In essence, the structure of your story is the process where the outline is transformed from being a simple idea to being the bones of your story. It becomes the part that holds the entire story up and gives it a form that is both natural, yet moving.

Where do Story Structures Come from?

Story structure is less of an invention or creation and more of an element of the story that was observed and thus plucked from the process and used as a tool to help generate new stories. For thousands of years, humans have been telling stories to one another whilst using story structure without ever knowing what it actually was. This is the part of the story that was used to draw listeners or readers forward through the story while keeping them actively engaged and wanting to know more. With the use of story structure, storytellers were able to walk people through the process of the story, rather than simply telling them the beginning and end factors. This meant that storytelling became an experience, both for the teller and the listener or reader. It was all thanks to story structure.

Although people weren't aware of what story structure actually was in the beginning, the idea of it emerged over time. It was identified as the structure of the story that was used to describe how certain characters within' the story dealt with problems and overcame them, as well as how they interacted with and communicated with other individuals from the story.

After identifying the concept of story structure and observing it from ancient storytelling experiences, people began using it as a general guideline for the process of building stories. Now, your story structure involves important information about the setting of your story, the people involved, the conflicts they experience, and how they overcome said conflicts. It is essentially every part of your story pulled together and planned out in a specific structure that helps you as the author understand what story you are trying to tell before and during the writing process.

Why You Need One

Having a story structure may seem pointless, especially if you already have the story in your head and you are simply attempting to get it out on paper. However, story structures are extremely valuable and can help you with the entire storytelling process. They are excellent for helping you identify how you are going to deliver the story to ensure that the reader receives the story effectively. This is more than simply providing the reader with information to help walk them from point a to point b. Instead, it is about giving them this relevant information in such a way that they are eager to know more and they stay actively engaged with the storytelling process.

When you design your story structure it helps you identify what your story sounds like to other people when they are reading it. It is important that you develop one before you start writing so that you have a strong execution plan going into the writing process. While you can simply write the story from your mind, this may result in you not emphasizing strong points enough, or otherwise diluting your story with information that takes away from it having a strong structure. Instead, you could plan your story out on paper first and essentially lay out the points that you will take your readers through within' the story. This way you can walk yourself through it and learn more about your story in advance. Doing this gives you the opportunity to identify any weak points and strengthen them, to ensure that your story makes sense and flows well, and to develop confidence in the idea that you have generated a strong enough plotline that your readers are going to stay actively engaged and enjoy the reading experience.

Now that you are more clear on what a story structure is and why it is so crucial to the writing process, it is time to explore the process of actually creating your own story structure so that you can embark on writing your own story. The following chapters will walk you through the step-by-step process of building your own story structure, as well as every technique you should know in order to have a strong structure that will leave your readers wanting more.

Chapter 2: The Essentials of Building a Structure

The first part of generating your own story structure is understanding the essentials. In this chapter, we are going to explore all of the basics that you should know when it comes to creating your own story structure. Throughout this chapter, you will be provided with tips and techniques to help you design the foundation of your structure. By the end, you should have a solid structure that will help you produce a phenomenal story.

9 Step Process

Most stories follow a typical nine-step process in order to generate their story structure. Some people prefer to alternate how the structure is designed, such as by introducing the climax in the first portion of the book. Still, they typically tend to break the book up into three main parts, or "acts" as they are called. This helps keep each part of the book focused on a certain subject that ultimately contributes to the overall story.

The following sections will introduce each step of the nine-step process and how they should be executed in order to produce a high-quality story structure. Please note that these are following the traditional method based on how many other stories have been structured throughout the ages. You may choose to alternate yours if you are more advanced, but if you are new to storytelling you will likely want to stick to and master this traditional structure before venturing into other structures. This will provide you with more practice towards developing a structure and using the purpose of the structure to your advantage. Once you are more skilled with structures then you can start to create alternative ones for your future stories because you will have a stronger idea about what makes them work and what doesn't.

Step One: First Act

The first step is to introduce the first act. This is the part of the story where you want to introduce the reader to your characters, the setting you have chosen, and anything that is at stake in the story. This is where they understand what is important and why. In the first act, you are given the opportunity to catch the attention of the reader and give them a reason to care about what story you are telling.

Example: You are writing a romance novel so you introduce the two lovers, as well as any other important characters to the reader. You will also take the time to provide insight as to where the book is taking place. This is where you can introduce the stakes as well, which essentially means you are telling the reader what is at stake and why it is important to the protagonist.

Step Two: The First Major Plot Point

The second step is to introduce the first major plot point to your reader. This should be defined by an event that takes place which forces the character to take action. You want this first major plot point to be considered the last scene in the first act so that readers are left wanting more. This is the finale of the first part of your book, so you want to leave it with some form of small cliffhanger. This both rewards the reader for reading by giving them some action to pay attention to, but also has them wondering what is going to come next as a result of the character's actions.

Example: The female character in your romance novel is walking home when an attacker tries to hurt her. The male character comes seemingly from nowhere and defends her honor, ensuring that she was protected and was not harmed by the attacker.

Step Three: First Half of Second Act

This is the part of the book where your character is coming back from the action they took at the end of the first act. Here you further explain what happened as a result of that plot point, as well as how your characters are dealing with it.

Example: As a result of him being the first to hit the attacker, despite him attempting to defend the female, the male role in your novel is being subjected to a criminal investigation. Because of this, he is trying to keep a low profile and avoid any further complications. The female is angry with the male for not calling the cops instead and allowing them to deal with it. She is

upset that he has subjected himself to the criminal investigation
through his actions, regardless of his reasoning.

Step Four: Second Major Plot Point

This is a plot point within' the story where the character who was attempting to regain their bearings from the first major plot point is forced back into action. Here, you want to work together with what said character has at stake to help the reader understand why they have been forced into action. Often the action is forced unto the character in the form of an ultimatum.

Example: Despite keeping a low profile for some time, the attacker returns and attempts to strike again. Only this time, he knows that the male is with the female and the attacker is attempting to force the male to act. He wants to have the male punished for attacking him, regardless of the fact that he was only attempting to protect her from the attacker. As a result, the male role is forced to decide between protecting her again or being faced with serious jail time. For the sake of these examples, let's say that he chooses to defend her honor once again.

Step Five: Second Half of Second Act

This is the part where all of the characters in the story begin to come into their own. Here, they are all grouping together to come against the antagonist. They are ensuring that the initial character is no longer left to take action on his or her own, but rather that they are supported by the other characters within' the story.

Example: This time, the female character is aware of what is going on and she is fighting to protect the male character. She is no longer angry with him for making the choice he made originally, and she is more willing to testify in his defense. They work together to get the attacker in trouble and to protect the male character through pleading that he was only practicing self-defense.

Step Six: Third Major Plot Point

This is where the protagonist's behavior appears to have led him or her to a place of defeat. In this part of the story, you want to introduce the idea that there may be no hope for this character and that they may be doomed because of the antagonistic forces. Here, they are beginning to feel as though they have hit rock bottom.

Example: Despite the female character testifying to the male character and fighting in his corner this time around, the court orders him guilty for assault. It appears that even though he was attempting to protect himself and the female character, no one is willing to see that. It seems there is no hope for him to avoid criminal charges altogether.

Step Seven: Third Act

In the third act, the protagonist is fighting against the antagonistic force as a last effort to take them down. Here they may not have total confidence that they can do it but they are not willing to give up just yet.

Example: The male character chooses to appeal the court ruling. Together, he and the female work to create a plan where they will prove that he is innocent and the attacker is the one who is truly guilty.

Step Eight: Climax

This is where there is a final face-off between the protagonist and antagonist. This is the deciding moment that is responsible for determining whether the story will end in favor of the antagonist, or in favor of the protagonist.

Example: The male character and the attacker face off in court. This is the part of the story that will determine whether the male is ruled guilty and is no longer welcome to appeal the charges, or whether the judge will see that he is actually innocent and it is the attacker who should be facing charges. For the sake of the example, we will say that it ends with the attacker being charged and the male being let off.

Step Nine: Resolution

This is where any loose ends from the story. It will also give insight to how the characters react to the climax and where they end up afterward. This is the wind down where readers are given the opportunity to know "what's next" and is required to avoid you from ending your book in a cliff-hanger.

Example: The female character is ecstatic that the male character is let free and they decide that they never want to risk facing a life without the other so they choose to get married.

As you can see, developing a strong story structure is important. Hopefully, through the use of the examples, you were able to understand how the structure lent a hand towards generating suspense and giving the reader a reason to keep reading. Because of how the story was structured and when certain pieces of information were revealed, the individual reading the story once it was complete would be engaged and would thus stay committed to reading the entire story so that they could discover how it ended.

It is important that you pay attention to the book in three sections as outlined above, as well as that you have a major plot point in each part. Dividing your story into three sections ensures that each part focuses on a particular element of the story and avoids you from going back and forth or otherwise introducing elements that are later forgotten about because you are not clear and focused on what you are writing. Having a major plot point in each section ensures that each section is rich and your reader is engaged the entire time. This is ultimately the structure you need in order to draw your reader forward and keep them moving through the story until they reach the end.

Chapter 3: Developing Your Story

Now that you are aware of what it takes to design a strong story structure, you may be wondering how you can develop a story that will fit with the structure! If you already have a general idea, then you can use the information from this section to help you strengthen that idea and ensure that all areas of your story are considered before them being structured and then written. If you have no idea as to what your story is going to be yet, use this chapter to help you identify a story and develop it so that it provides you with plenty of material to write your book about.

Study Existing Plots

When you are working towards developing your story one of the best ways to go about it is to read. Reading other people's stories gives you the opportunity to see what worked and what didn't, and it also provides you with inspiration to enrich your own story. While you don't want to be plagiarizing or stealing stories from other people, getting inspiration to enrich your own and strengthen the plot is always a great idea. This ensures that you are going to have a really strong story that provides enough material to engage your audience and keep them captive for the duration of the book.

When you are studying other people's stories you want to do more than just read them. You want to pay attention to who the characters are, how they develop throughout the novel, how the events take place including when and where, and all locations that the story takes place in. You should also identify the sequence that the locations are used in. Knowing more about these primary areas of the story allows you to get an idea of how books are written and what authors do in order to develop their own storyline. You can see the techniques in action and understand how they contribute to the overall experience being delivered in the story.

Draft Up Your Plot

When you are designing your plot there are some strategies you can use to see your plot come together without writing out the entire story first. The best way to do this is through drafting up your plot. You can do this by writing a paragraph or two from each ideal chapter and then read them in order. While it will obviously be missing many details, doing this will give you an idea of how the plot points flow together and if they are strong enough to give you plenty of writing material to work with.

Using a plotting strategy like this gives you the opportunity to look at your plot as a whole and make sure that it works effectively in the story you are writing. This helps you see what areas of the plot are rich and which aren't. You can also finalize the main plot sequencing and points before starting the writing process so that you are certain that it is in the order that you want and that it all works well together. This essentially gives you a birds-eye view of what your structure is and lets you know whether or not it works.

Create a Timeline

A great way to build your story is to create a timeline. This timeline should include all of the major plot points in chronological order. Seeing these together helps you identify how each one builds into the next one and makes sure that they work well together. If anything is missing or you feel there is a plot point that does not fit well in the overall story, then you can use this as an opportunity to eliminate it.

Similar to drafting your plot, creating a timeline allows you to take a birds-eye view at the work you have created and determine whether or not it works. The more you pay attention to the structure of your story from different elements now, the more you can be certain that it will work and produce a strong story in the long run.

Plan Character Development Along the Plot Line

After you have generated your plot draft and your timeline, take your characters into consideration. Pay attention to how you want them to develop along the storyline. It is natural for characters to change throughout stories, and even necessary in order for the story to progress. A great way to plan their development is to plan it alongside the story development. How is the development of the story going to contribute to the growth of the character? Consider this while you are deciding how your character will develop along the way.

Change the 5 "W's

A great way to ensure that you have developed the story strong enough is to check that you have changed the five w's along the way. The who, what, when, where, and why of the story should all develop or completely change along the progression of your story. In real life, these change from moment to moment and day to day. If you want your story to be realistic and relatable, you need to ensure that they are changed in your story as well.

If you want to take your story from good to great, these answers should not be simple and direct. Each one should have a series of answers that guide the element from the start of the book to the end. They should change in a way that convinces the reader that the change was natural and realistic, and helps the character feel as though it is a true story being told. Think back to your own day, for example you may have woken up in your home and now you are sitting in a coffee shop reading this book. You may have woken in a bad mood and now you are in a better one, or vice versa. The reasons as to why your mood change are also important to the story of your day. Who was involved in your day and what helped you pass the day by will have also changed from moment to moment. Just like your day naturally progressed as a story of its own, you need your story to progress in the same way. This ensures that your book goes in-depth enough to make it convincing to your reader. If any of the five w's are not developed enough, look for opportunities to strengthen them so that your story will be rich and full of realistic details.

Design a Story Board

Creating a storyboard is another great way to look at the structure of your story. A great way to create the storyboard is to write each major plot point and important element on a cue card or post it so that they can easily be moved around to create the final story map. This gives you a great opportunity to see how each event works together and organize them effortlessly without having to scratch out things and replace them everywhere.

Consider Subplots

Creating subplots that fit in seamlessly with your overall story is a great way to enrich the story experience and add more depth to it while also encouraging reader engagement. Subplots are essentially the "what else" part of the story. For example, if you are writing a book about the main character who is seeking justice, consider including elements of why this justice is so important for this character. Perhaps they want the criminal incarcerated because he or she deserves to be, but it may also be because the protagonist has allowed others to walk all over him for too long and he is ready to stand up for himself. Therefore, getting justice is both about having justice served *and* about building the confidence to actually fight for what is right.

Subplots are an incredible story developing strategy that can help you create a story that is much richer in context. You can include as many or as few subplots as you want, but make sure that each one makes sense to the overall story itself. They should work together with the main plot, rather than going against it or straying away from it completely.

Incorporate Driven Elements

All of the best stories incorporate one specific element that enables the story to be so great. That is the element of change. In order to create change, there are two very specific things you need. Character-driven and action-driven elements to your story. These elements are two things that can help incorporate change into your story in such a way that yours fosters all of the greatness that all of the other best titles do.

The reason why change is so powerful in a story is that that is what drives the story forward. People are curious to know about how characters change and grow throughout the course of the story every bit as much as they are interested in learning about how the story develops itself. People do not want to read a story about static characters who do the same thing every day and nothing changes. That would be extremely boring and would lead to them closing the book and turning away from it entirely. Think about it, would you read a book like that? Likewise, people are not interested in a book that has minimal change, or where the change only occurs on one very specific thing. Instead, people want to see the entire story change. They want to see the characters grow, they want to see the circumstances evolve, and they want to see the protagonist, and even the antagonist, end up somewhere completely different from where they were when the story changed. Incorporating as much natural and realistic change as possible helps drive your story forward and keep it both interesting and engaging.

As previously mentioned, there are two different types of change you can use to drive your story forward: character-driven change, and action-driven change. Both of these elements should be included in your own story if you want a diverse and realistic story that will help keep your readers engaged and reading your book all the way until the last page.

Character-driven change is used by showing the stakes the character has. For example, their child, their family, their significant other, their career. By incorporating these stakes and giving the reader insight as to why they are so important to the character, you can use them as an opportunity to drive the story forward. The most important thing to understand is that without character-driven change, there is no story. Character-driven change is essentially the answer to "why" your character is doing anything that takes place in the story. This explains why they will do almost anything, even stuff that seems highly irrational or nonsensical, in various situations. "Because my child is sick" or, "because I could lose my job" for example, would be the stakes and therefore would answer "why" the character is so invested in something. By creating this type of explanation and therefore emotional attachment from the reader to the character, and furthermore the character's stakes, you can make virtually every part of the story that much more engaging and interesting for your reader. Without character-driven change, your readers are not given an opportunity to understand why they need to care about the events taking place in your book.

Action-driven change is an entirely different form of change. This is the change whereby specific actions happen that cause the story to drive forward. High-speed chases, break-ins, getting arrested, being put on the chopping block at work, the spouse falling in love with someone else, the kid getting into trouble, all of these would constitute as action-drive changes. For the most part, these are actions that are taking place that cannot be stopped or influenced by your protagonist. Instead, the protagonist must find a way to respond and react to these actions.

When you use character-driven change effectively, action-driven change becomes that much more intriguing and engaging for your reader. Because they understand the stakes and have developed an emotional attachment to your characters, they are much more concerned with the action, as well as the outcome. It is important that you use a balanced amount of both types of changes in your story. This will help you round out your story and keep it moving forward without being too heavily charged in one direction or another. Furthermore, you want to make sure that you don't go overboard on the change. While it does drive the story forward, you want to make sure that you use it in a very realistic and natural manner. This helps the reader relate to the story and believe it, instead of feeling as though it is completely unlikely and therefore it is not relatable. If a reader cannot relate to a story in one way or another, they are not going to continue reading it because it will be too unbelievable for them.

Question Yourself

When you are in the process of developing your story, make sure you question yourself a lot along the way. The more you question yourself, your intentions, the story and the plot line, the more you can develop it. Questioning it ultimately gives you the opportunity to see where any loopholes may lie, if any part of the plot is weak, or if there is any reason that you should need to develop part of the story more. It also helps you identify where there may be too much action or development going on so that you can scale it back. If you are not taking the time to question yourself and your story structure, you may be missing important things that could take away from the value of your story altogether.

Some great questions to ask yourself include ones such as:

- Why has the character changed, how did the change happen, and what was the purpose of this change?

- How much has the character changed since the beginning of the story?

- Is the change natural and believable?

- What has each plot point taught the characters, thus teaching them about the story's primary situation or conflict?

- Can you identify some core themes within' the story? Are there too many or too few core themes taking place?

- Is the story believable? Does it flow naturally?

- Does the story move forward effectively, or is it too slow?

Asking yourself these questions will help ensure that each part of your story structure is strong and that it will help you produce a believable, relatable, and enjoyable story that is interesting and engaging. If you find that your answer is "no" or "I don't know" to any of the questions above, take the time to further explore that question and find ways that you can strengthen the story structure itself.

Get Feedback

Finally, it is important that you take the time to get feedback on your story structure. As with most things, having someone else take a look and give you some insight as to where the strengths and weaknesses lie and if any adaptations or alterations should be made means that nothing will be missed. This is the best way to make sure that you have a strong structure going into your story that will both serve you and serve your readers by giving you enough material and answers to generate an interesting an engaging story.

If you do not personally know someone who can provide you with feedback, there are many online platforms and forums that you can turn to where you can find someone to help you with looking over the structure. Furthermore, you can also look to find someone from your ideal target audience and have them look over the structure for you. Regardless of who you get to help you with the structure, do your best to make sure it is someone who is either in or thoroughly understands your target audience, and ideally someone with some experience in story structure. Having someone who intimately knows you are trying to reach and what you are trying to say can help significantly as it ensures that any feedback or critique they provide you with is accurate and helpful. Those who are unclear on the audience you are trying to reach or who have zero understanding of story structure or what is required in order to make a good book may not be able to provide you with information that will help you improve your structure. In fact, they may even have you questioning parts that you should not need to question. It is important that the person you choose to work with understands your needs.

Chapter 4: Creating Suspense

Regardless of what genre you are writing for, you need to be skilled in creating suspense for your story. Suspense is the element that keeps readers wondering what is coming next and how events are going to unfold. When used properly, suspense can be what draws one plot point to the next. If you want to create a compelling and convincing fiction novel that encourages readers to continue reading, you are going to need to master the art of creating suspense. The next ten tips are about how you can begin creating suspense in your own novel to keep your readers wanting more.

Understand Your Genre

Before you begin creating suspense, it is important that you understand the genre you are writing in. Each genre uses suspense differently to draw characters forward and keep readers coming back. If you want to do your book justice, you need to practice using suspense for your unique genre.

Let's take a look at three different types of novels and where the suspense would come into play for each type.

Mystery: A horror or major event takes place in the first chapter and the rest of the book is spent figuring out why the event occurred and who was responsible for it. For example, the protagonist's spouse was killed in the first chapter and the rest of the book is spent uncovering who was responsible.

Romance: You build up to the point where the two lovers finally get together. The climax, or the two getting together, officially takes place later in the book, usually within' the last couple of chapters. For example, two lovers know they're meant to be together but the timing never seems right. One is always dating someone else when the other is available for the relationship to work. As a result, they are never able to get together until the end when they finally make it work.

Suspense: The knowledge of an impending horror is upon the characters in the novel and they spend the entire time trying to avoid it until they can no longer keep it from happening. For example, someone knows they are going to jail for embezzlement but doesn't know when. This character knows that he has been tracked and that the FBI is well aware of what has been going on. He does not know when he will be taken down, but it will happen.

Provide Adequate Viewpoints

When it comes to developing a strong case of suspense in your novel, you need to give the reader adequate knowledge. This comes from providing them with different viewpoints. Through this, you can give them insight to the protagonist's side of things, and the antagonist's side of things. The best way to get a lot of suspense building in your book is by giving your reader insight as to what is going to happen before the protagonist knows. This gives the writer the opportunity to increase the emotional attachment to the protagonist and the stakes. The reader is drawn along an experience where they know what is yet to come but they have to watch the protagonist find out and learn the consequences of certain actions. The tension that builds on the reader because of what they know that the protagonist doesn't know is similar to someone who has a secret they're not allowed to tell. It engages the reader and makes them want to know more and to understand where the book will end up.

Put Time on Your Side

Time is an incredible tool when it comes to writing a book with suspense. You want to use time on your side so that you can increase the amount of suspense in the novel. Time gives you the opportunity to make the reader feel as though the protagonist is working against the clock. Everything they are doing should have some form of time constraint on it. Ideally, it should appear as though the clock is working in favor of the antagonist or antagonistic force to keep the suspense strong. For example, if you were writing a mystery novel about a murder that took place, it should seem as though the protagonist doesn't have enough time to find the murderer. Perhaps there is some jurisdiction law that states that if the person is not found within' a set amount of time the charges won't be as strong, or the murderer has been leaving clues that they have left town and it gets harder and harder to find who they are. Several dead end leads are exhausted before the protagonist finally discovers who the murderer was in the end. Putting time on your side lets you build suspense by creating the illusion that something won't happen, even though it needs to.

Keep The Stakes High

The stakes that you use in a story should be high enough to justify a high amount of suspense. The higher the stakes the more pressing the need to protect them is, both in the mind of the character and the reader. While you don't need to choose devastating stakes that are excessively high, picking ones that someone would actually be desperate to protect will ensure that your reader understands why the protagonist is so passionate about protecting their stakes. Some examples would include an executive who is facing being exposed for shady business dealings, therefore costing them their job and their reputation and making them unlikeable for other employers. Or, perhaps a male is in love with a female in a romance novel, but he grows tired of waiting for her to make up her mind so he pursues a relationship with someone else. She realizes she wants him more than anything but must figure out a way to tell him, and fast, before he marries the other person or realizes that he does not want to be with her altogether. Alternatively, you may choose to write a story about someone with a powerful societal position being murdered and they must find out who did it before they strike another powerful member of society. By keeping the stakes high but reasonable, you make it very clear as to why your reader needs to be so concerned with what is taking place in the book. The stronger your stakes are, the more your reader will be passionate alongside your character to ensure that they are not lost.

Don't Be Afraid to Apply Pressure

Pressure is a great way to add suspense to any novel. The odds should be stacked well against your character and it should take a great amount of effort and energy for them to tip the odds in their favor and save the day. The more the odds are stacked against them, the higher the pressure is and therefore the more you can draw the reader to wondering if they will ever be able to beat the odds. When they finally do, the reader and character alike will feel a great deal of relief from the experience.

When you are writing about creating pressure, make sure that you never lead your protagonist right to the breaking point. They should bend and cripple under pressure, but they should never stop pushing. You should ensure that they are always pushed *almost* too far so that they have *just* enough amount of energy to push back and it is at that time that they finally beat the antagonistic force and experience success in their heroic attempts.

Make Use of Dilemmas

Dilemmas are a great way to increase suspense in a story and have your reader highly engaged. Dilemmas present a "this or that" action for the character. They should be forced into action, and make sure that the pressure is on for it to happen fast. When dilemmas are being thrown towards your character it is important to make sure that they are being thrown by the antagonist most often. This should present the idea that the protagonist cannot win in the situation. For example, for them to save one character another must die, they can either lose their family and save their job or lose their job and save their family, or even indulging in alcohol after swearing to sobriety at some point within' the novel.

When you are presenting dilemmas, make sure that the antagonist always crosses the line. Because they are the villain, they shouldn't even think twice about going across it. However, the protagonist should always be forced with their morals and values. Should they do one, or the other? Which will be the less of two evils? Is there a way that they can make the best of both horrible situations? True to heroic nature, they should be struggling to find the answer to the dilemma.

One great reason why dilemmas work is because you can apply pressure and time constraints so that the protagonist is forced to make a decision fast, which puts pressure on him and gets the reader worried about what is going to happen. Using these three strategies together is a great way to build suspense throughout your book.

Complicate Things

You don't need to restrict to just presenting your protagonist with one or even two conflicts at any given time. Instead, feel free to pile on the complications every now and again. The more complicated things get, the more difficult it will be for them to come up with the solution and make the right choice. At times, it should feel like the protagonist is trying to juggle several balls at once and he is just barely keeping them from dropping every time. This is a great time to push the protagonist almost to the point of breaking before bringing them back in for a final and much awaited victory.

Avoid Becoming Predictable

When your book runs too smoothly, it becomes predictable. It also becomes uninteresting and the readers struggle to relate to it. Life is not about being smooth and predictable. Most often we are all living in a hot mess where we are balancing many different things and trying to stay afloat along the way. If you want to write a great book, it should be similar to this. Throw random curveballs in, take a spin somewhere where one wasn't expected, and have your reader surprised at some of the elements that are being tossed in, and when. When it comes to writing, don't let the hero rely on the idea that everything will go in their favor. In fact, almost nothing should. This way when it finally does, it will come as a surprise. Furthermore, your antagonist shouldn't go with everything going in their way, either. Let both of them face challenges, twists and turns along the way. The more they are affected by curveballs and unexpected experiences, the more realistic the story will be. Make the protagonist slip up and result in an almost-victory instead of a true victory, and let the antagonist fail at the most inconvenient of times for them. This keeps your readers on their toes and unsure about what is going to happen, when.

Develop Your Villain

Your villain is the antagonistic force in your book, and they need to be developed really well. Your reader should be mentally pushing against the villain, and rooting for the hero. As a result, you need to have a really well developed villain that has the reader truly believing and feeling as though they are a nasty force to be reckoned with.

Make sure that you use the right villain for your novel genre, as well. In a mystery, for example, it should not be clear as to who the villain is until the end. With a romance novel on the other hand, the villain might be time itself, or the person coming between the two lovers and keeping them apart. Alternatively, in a suspense novel the villain should be highly visible at all times and people should ultimately just be wondering when they will finally strike. The more you understand what type of villain is appropriate for your unique genre, the easier it will be to create one that is believable and extremely well developed.

When you develop your antagonist, make sure that you are very specific on who they are and what makes them tick. You want this character to be so developed that your reader feels as though they personally know them. Furthermore, your antagonist should change throughout the story, which is easiest to prove if your reader knows who they are from how you've written about them.

Develop Your Hero

In addition to developing your villain, you need to develop your hero. This is the one that finally defeats the antagonistic force and creates the victory of the story. The best way to create a strong hero is to really build on the character and give the reader plenty of reasons to love them. This is the character your reader is going to follow throughout the story. This is who they will be rooting for, worrying for, and curious about. They want to know everything they can about this character, and they have mentally prepared themselves to be on their side emotionally. Therefore, you need to use this character to not only build an emotional attachment between your reader and your protagonist, but also to use that attachment to manipulate the emotions of your reader. The protagonist is the character that you are going to leverage in order to get your reader nervous, curious, excited, happy, sad, angry, and any other emotion you want them to engage in throughout the experience. The best way to do that is to have a well-developed character that your reader can truly feel as though they have befriended.

Chapter 5: Additional Story Structure Tips

In addition to tips on basic story structure, developing a strong story, and how to create suspense, there are many other great tips that can help you when it comes to story structures. Now that you have the three important elements down, you can explore additional tips that will take you further into the realm of pro writer and help you generate a story that is going to be fantastic. The following tips are provided from real authors who have experience in writing their own high quality fiction materials. By following these tips, you can ensure that you don't only have a great story structure, but a phenomenal one.

Research Different Story Structures

Although there is a basic system that virtually all structures follow, it is important to understand that there are many modifications and alterations made to this structure in true writing. After all, if every story followed the basic structure down to the last detail then there would be no point in reading. We would be able to read the first chapter and know exactly how a book was going to turn out. By making modifications to the structure and playing it around in different ways, writers have the ability to stick to a structure that works while also providing a script that is unique, unpredictable, and engaging for readers.

Armed with this knowledge, you can prepare yourself to start researching many different story structures. The best way is to read other people's novels and do your best to identify the structure within' them. As you are reading, write down the major plot points and other key details that come into play with these plot points. Doing this will help you identify a series of structures that are used to create incredible novels, and how the writers spun them to work for the story. Do this several times over and pay attention to patterns that arise. Then, choose the structure you like most and make it work for your novel!

Stick to Structures that Are Traditional for Your Genre

For the best results, it is important that you stick to structures that are traditional to your genre. Although this may sound like a surefire way to create a story that sounds like every other story in the genre, it actually isn't. You will learn more about why in a moment. In the meantime, it is important that you understand why it is a good idea to stick to these traditional structures.

Each structure is designed to create a different effect for the story. Some build suspense, some build mystery, and some build both. Depending on what genre you are writing for, you are going to want to go for a structure that provides you with the right elements of virtually everything. These are going to be elements of suspense, story building opportunities, character development opportunities, and more. Each genre tends to be told in a unique way because it achieves a specific result. Therefore, each structure that is unique to each genre is built to help achieve that specific result. For example, you wouldn't want to use a suspense structure for a mystery novel because you would thus be identifying the perpetrator immediately. Likewise, you wouldn't want to use a mystery structure in a suspense novel because it would destroy the element of suspense by not giving enough information to the reader.

It is important that you do not reinvent the wheel, but rather you explore the different styles of wheels that exist for your market. Furthermore, just because you are limited to only using structures that are traditional for your genre does not mean that there is only one single structure you can follow. Each genre has its own selection of structures that will and won't work. The best way to identify which one you want to use is to read them, as described in the previous section, and pay attention to each type of structure you come across. As you do, identify which one would work best for your unique story and enlist that as your structure of choice.

Structure the Novel to Your Central Theme

As you are designing the structure for your novel, make sure that you are conforming the structure to fit the central theme of your novel and not the other way around. You never want to be derailing or detracting from the story as an attempt to stick to your structure. Remember, a structure is supposed to be a guideline that gets you to where you need to go. You do not have to follow it down to every last detail in order for your story to be a good one. Instead, you want to pay attention to the story structure and write your novel with that structure in mind.

Stories that are written to strictly to the guidelines set out in the structure end up sounding very forced and uncomfortable. Readers will often lose engagement quickly because the story becomes predictable and unnatural. They cannot relate to the story so they do not want to read it any longer. Ultimately, it takes away from the reader's experiences and kills the chance of your novel being greater.

To elaborate on how the structure *should* be used, we will explore how exactly you can enforce its guidelines. One of the biggest things you want to pay attention to, and use your structure for, is to ensure that your book stays focused on the central theme. If your novel strays too far away from the central theme at any given point, it may take away from the story overall. You never want to over share or get off track on a topic that does not contribute to the central theme or purpose of your novel. This is where your story structure comes in handy. Having a structure that can help keep you on track is highly valuable as it ensures that you do not derail your story and end up with a novel about love that gets too off track and ends up being about one person's career, or something else. Essentially you want to employ your story structure as a guide to keep you on track and to build a strong story, but you do not want to follow it so closely that you snuff out the quality of your story and produce something generic and predictable.

Modify the Template to Suit Your Plot

To expand further on the previous tip, it is important to work on modifying your template to suit your plot. Although you do not want to create an entirely new structure for your novel, or take one from the wrong genre, this does not mean that you cannot modify the template. For example, if you would prefer a certain plot point to happen sooner rather than later, or vice versa, you certainly have creative freedom to make this decision. Remember, you are a storyteller and your story is your work of art. Just because there are certain methods to use doesn't mean you can't get creative. For example, paint brushes are what you are *supposed* to paint with, but many choose to paint with sponges or even rags instead. Some even use a different material altogether, and yet the art is still incredible beautiful. In fact, it may be even more beautiful because of the unique method used. In this analogy, a different approach was used but the same bare basic structure was used: a tool was used to pick up paint and apply it to a canvas. You can easily modify certain parts of that, such as by changing your tools or picking a unique canvas, but at the very root is the same structure. The same goes for writing.

Just because authors before you have always used a specific template doesn't mean you cannot modify that template to suit your story. If you find that certain elements would serve better at a different area in the story, you are always welcome to do that. The best thing you can do as a writer is exercise your creative freedom. When you let loose from expectations and open yourself up to generate phenomenal content, inevitably you generate phenomenal content. As long as you stick to the bare bones basics with your structure, you are going to end up with a great story. If on the off chance you don't, it is a great opportunity to further research the structure and understand where you went wrong and how you could create a better story and structure in the future.

Create the Structure First, Modify it Later

It is always a good idea to begin your story with a strong structure. That being said, you should seek to create the structure before you begin writing. Having your structure created first and then creating a story around that structure helps ensure that you are staying on track with the basics. However, that does not mean that you are restricted to only writing to that specific structure.

As writers carry along the process of writing, they often find that it takes them down a natural path and therefore certain elements of their original structure no longer serve the story as powerfully as they could. The best thing to do in this circumstances is to reevaluate the structure and modify it so that it better suits the story in the direction that you have taken it. When you do this, you open yourself up to the opportunity of creating something much more powerful than you originally set out to do.

Creating a story is not always as straightforward as it seems. In many cases you will go into it with a very specific idea of what you want the story to be like and as a result of your writing process you discover that it actually works for reasons other than you thought so it naturally evolves away from your initial intentions. The best thing you can do in these circumstances is honor that natural evolution in your story and work with it. If you try and go against it in order to stick to your original structure you may end up creating a strange and unnatural twist backward, or it will otherwise not flow well. In order to give yourself creative freedom while also holding on to some sense of direction, the best thing to do is to start with a structure and modify it if your story evolves away from the initial structure you laid out for it. This will keep you on track while also giving you the potential to create an incredible story.

Hide the Structure in Your Writing

When it comes to the writing process, you want to ensure that you are hiding the structure within' your writing. It should not be painfully obvious what structure you have used. If it is, then your story will become predictable and people will lose interest. Virtually every story structure has been used several times over. This means that people will have a pretty easy ability to link your strategies together and determine what the novel will end like regardless of whether or not they have read it. They will also likely discover what major plot points are going to occur well before they ever happen. When the book becomes this predictable, it also becomes highly uninteresting.

A great writer knows how to hide the structure within' the story. Make things happen sooner or later than expected, twist away from the structure here and there to blend it in, and do your best to avoid going very clearly from point one to point two. You want your readers to question what is happening and be surprised along the way. Give them the idea that they have already arrived at the major plot point with one activity and then blow them out of the water with something much bigger. Keep the element of surprise active and use it as your weapon to bury the structure. The less obvious your structure is, the more unpredictable your story becomes and therefore the more power you have as the author to keep your reader engaged and have them wanting to learn more about what you have yet to tell them.

Keep Your Structure Organized and Handy

For a practical writing tip in regards to your structure, it is important that you keep it organized and that it is available at all times when you are writing. Your structure will prove to be a highly valuable tool when it comes to producing your novel. Being able to refer back to it at different points and identify where you are at will help you know where to go with your story, as well as help you stay focused on the central theme and overall purpose of your book.

A great way to keep your structure handy and useful during the writing process is to have it written down somewhere, such as on cue cards, and nearby whenever you are writing. This way you can identify where you have already been on the structure and where you have yet to go. It will also provide you with the ability to refer back to it regularly, as well as effortlessly revise it as needed. The reason why you might want to make your "final" structure on cue cards is because if you choose to modify it along the way you can easily do it without having to completely start over or rewrite it. This makes it effortless for you to modify it as needed and keep the parts you want.

Experiment

There is nothing more valuable than hands-on practice when it comes to any hobby, and this fact is not lost on writing. If you are looking for an opportunity to create an incredible book, take any chance you have to experiment. There are many ways that you can experiment when it comes to writing, and each can help you increase your understanding of story structures and how they work into the overall book, as well as how you can use your unique writing style to make the most of your story structure.

One great method is to take note of a few different story structures that will work effectively for the genre you are writing in and then draft your story out based on these. This means that you want to write a few paragraphs on each part of the structure and then read them together. It will give you the opportunity to see how your story would work together and if you have generated a strong enough story structure for your book. Another method is to practice writing short stories with different structures in a smaller way. While you won't be able to pack as much into the story as you would with a novel, it will give you a better idea of how your novel would sound with each unique structure in place.

Experimentation is the best way to practice writing and get an idea for what you like and what you don't like. If you are serious about it and you have time, practicing writing each novel with different structures and employing different strategies is a great way to see each structure in action and get a feel for how it works for your books. You can identify how the structure serves your story and where it might be weak, as well as how you can embed the structure within' the story using unique writing strategies to hide it from plain sight. This is a great way to practice writing overall and increase your skill if you are interested and have the time to invest.

Take Notes

Finally, a great method to use when it comes to learning and growing as a writer or as virtually anything is to take notes. When you are reading other books, take notes on what you like and don't like about the book, particularly when it comes to the structure of the book. When you are writing your own books, pay attention to where you have struggled and where you are succeeding. On the points where you a struggling, explore ways that you could make it easier. When it comes to each unique structure, write down how it serves your story and any thoughts you might have about how it could be better next time, or when you go through the editing process.

Taking notes allows you to review what you have already thought and felt about certain experiences with your story and its structure and gives you something easy and finite to look back on. When you take notes it means that you are not going to forget about or lose your thoughts in the process. This means that you can hold onto them and make the necessary changes without having to attempt to remember what it was that you wanted to do in the first place.

There are many great strategies you can use to strengthen your story structure immediately, as well as to help you increase your skills and become a better story writer through your structure over time. The more you emphasize on learning this skill now, the greater you will be at is as you go on. Remember that a strong structure can truly make or break a story. A bad structure equals a bad story, a good one equals a good story and a great structure will return you a great story. If you want to be great, you have to practice being great from the start. Over time and with practice you will graduate from being great to being phenomenal!

Conclusion

Thank you for reading *"Story Structure: Step-by-Step | Essential Story Building, Story Development and Suspense Writing Tricks Any Writer Can Learn"*. This book was designed to assist you in learning everything you need to know about story structures, including how you can make an incredible one.

I hope this book was able to elaborate on the concept of story structures, including what they are and why they are important. I also hope that you were able to learn plenty about how you can create your own story structure, develop your story, create suspense, and ultimately strengthen the structure of your story in order to create a phenomenal book.

The next step is to build your story structure and use it alongside the creation of your new book. Take your time and follow the steps within' this book to ensure that you have a strong structure that will serve you in the process of creating your book. Remember, as you go about the writing process you will want to check back to your structure to ensure that you are sticking to your original plan. However, if you find that your structure is no longer serving the overall creation of your story, you can always modify your structure for stronger impact. Sometimes the writing process can alter our plans and take us down a separate natural path. If this happens, ensure that you use the structure to support your story and the other way around.

Thank you!

PLOTTING

STEP-BY-STEP

ESSENTIAL STORY PLOTTING, CONFLICT WRITING AND PLOTLINE TRICKS ANY WRITER CAN LEARN

SANDY MARSH

BOOK 5: PLOTTING

STEP-BY-STEP

Essential Story Plotting, Conflict Writing and Plotline Tricks Any Writer Can Learn

Sandy Marsh

reparation, damages, or monetary loss due to the information herein, either directly or indirectly.

Respective authors own all copyrights not held by the publisher.

The information herein is offered for informational purposes solely and is universal as so. The presentation of the information is without a contract or any type of guarantee assurance.

The trademarks that are used are without any consent, and the publication of the trademark is without permission or backing by the trademark owner. All trademarks and brands within this book are for clarifying purposes only and are the owned by the owners themselves, not affiliated with this document.

Table of Contents

Introduction

Thank you and congratulations for purchasing *"Plotting: Step-by-Step | Essential Story Plotting, Conflict Writing and Plotline Tricks Any Writer Can Learn"*.

In this book, we are going to further explore how you can write a rich plot that will not only give you plenty of material to write about but will also give you a depth of material that takes your story to the next level. The goal of designing a plotline is to establish a rich story that will intrigue your readers and give you, as the writer, the opportunity to have maximum impact on your storytelling process. Through creating a strong and productive plotline, you give yourself the power to take your story to greater heights and leave your readers with more to take away from the story itself in terms of lessons, experience, and entertainment.

Throughout this book, you are going to learn more about how you can write your own plot in such a way that will help you achieve those next-level results. You will learn about the basic structure of a plotline, as well as how you can build your own plot around this structure. Then, you will be guided through the process of taking your plot outline and bringing it to life in such a way that enables you to use this plotline for maximum impact. Finally, you will learn about some tips and tricks straight from the pros of story writing themselves. In this final chapter, you will be provided with everything you need to tie up any loose ends and make sure that you have a rock solid plotline that will drive your story forward in the most powerful, rewarding, and non-expecting ways possible.

If you are ready to learn how you can create the best plotline ever, and how you can execute it in your writing process so that it has maximum impact, then you are in the right place. Please take your time and build your plot alongside this book so that you can take in every piece of advice being offered and apply it to your own plot building practice. This will ensure that you are benefiting from all of the knowledge within' this book and that you have the best possible results. And of course, enjoy!

Chapter 1: A Basic Plot Outline

Plot outlines, like with story outlines and story structures, have a specific sequence that they are usually created in. While you can choose to alter the timing of this sequence, it is always best that you stick to the sequence itself. This will ensure that you are using the proper and best outline available to help you create a rich and powerful plot. In this chapter, you are going to explore what this basic outline is, as well as every element that exists in this outline. You will also gain an understanding as to why the structure is built this way, and how this contributes to your successful story plot. By the end, you should have a strong understanding as to how this structure works, why it works, and how it looks in stories when it has been executed effectively.

What is the Purpose of The Plot Outline?

Like with all of the elements of your story that we have discussed until now, the plot outline or plot diagram has a very profound and powerful purpose when it comes to your story writing process and experience. This tool is specifically used to help you choose major plot points and organize them along a story arc so that you can identify what your story will be like beforehand. The reason you do this is for several reasons, though it is primarily for the purpose of organizing your plot sequencing so that the story pans out in a strong, chronological manner that allows it to flow efficiently and effectively.

Many people believe that using something such as a plot outline will restrict the writing process and prevent them from having creative freedom and expression when it comes to writing the novel. There are many ways to help further open up the opportunity for creative expression, but ultimately this is not the case. Having a plot outline does not need to mean that you specifically plan out each minor element of your book before you get to the writing process. Instead, it gives you the opportunity to get an overall idea of where you are going with your novel and how you can get there while providing and delivering the best story possible. This is more about embracing your creative freedom and using it to guide you towards a story that leaves a massive impact on your readers than it is about eliminating your creative freedom and forcing you to think about all of the details *right now* rather than as they come to you.

Plot outlines serve as a great backbone to your story. These provide the bare bone basics of your story, what you want to include in it, and how you want to deliver it to your readers. As you are writing, you still have the power to switch things around, including enormous amounts of creativity in the actual writing process, and otherwise, add your own personal touch to your novel. Having the plot outline simply means that you know what general direction to head in and when and where things should happen within' your book so that you are capable of delivering a strong story that has the ability to engage, impress, and excite your readers, no matter what genre you are writing in.

What the Outline Looks Like

The outline looks somewhat like an unfinished triangle or the moving chart that gathers information on a person's heartbeat.

It starts out as a flat line, spikes up to create a triangular shape, and then comes back down to the flat line. This is the most basic plot outline that exists, and it is the one that virtually every story follows. Although you may slightly alter where the spike exists on your own diagram, or how much rising action and falling action exist before and after the spike, the shape remains generally untouched, and it serves as an excellent representation of what your plot outline should look like. Because of the shape of this spike, it is also known as a story arc.

Where the plotline starts, with the flatline, is known as an exposition. This is the beginning of your novel, and it serves by providing you with the opportunity to introduce your characters and the other important elements of the book. This is where you want to introduce the setting of your novel, the stakes that your character(s) are concerned about, and what the problem is. It is through this that you gain the momentum within your novel that will allow you to accelerate towards the problem while keeping your reader engaged, as here is where you give them a reason to care and have the interest to keep reading what you have written.

Once you have successfully completed the exposition, you want to introduce the rising action. This is the part of the story where you practice suspense-building techniques to keep your reader engaged and involved. You are using this part of the book to climb towards the climax of the story. Here, the problem that your character(s) are facing is getting worse, and the complications are exceeding. Usually, this rising action takes course over many pages and even chapters so that you can generate a large element of suspense before you eventually arrive at the climax. Here, you can introduce problems and solve them all well before reaching the actual climax. The primary purpose is to draw the story up to where "it" happens, with "it" being the big reason why you are telling the story in the first place.

The climax is usually around the middle of the story, though it can take place sooner or later depending on how you have chosen to write the story and where you have introduced each unique plot element. This is the most exciting and typically most rewarding part of the story, especially for readers, because it gives them satisfaction after all of the rising action you have shared with them until now. This is the part that makes the reader question "what's next?" and want to keep reading to find out.

Once you have worked through the climax of your story, you officially fall into a decline otherwise known as falling action. This is where the "what now?" part of the climax is revealed as you give your reader an idea of what the resolution is following the climax of your story. You use this as an opportunity to tie up loose ends, to explain where things go after the climax, and to give your reader an opportunity to reflect on the rest of the story. You answer any questions that may have been left behind throughout the rest of the story and generally work towards closing *most* things off in this area. This is where you are working towards the resolution.

The end of the story is also known as the resolution, and this is where the resolution is actually identified. You use this part of the book to inform your reader as to how the resolution has affected each character, how things have turned out for them, and where they are now that the story's problem has been resolved. You close up all of the final loose ends here and provide answers to any unanswered questions. This is where you ultimately provide closure for your book, your characters, and your reader.

Following this plot outline or diagram gives you the opportunity to use a story arc that works. Virtually every story is built along this diagram in one way or another. Sometimes the climax takes place sooner or later than the center of the story, but this is typically how books are written. This outline is used because it works, but also because it gives you a structured outline to help you write the information that your readers need in order for the story to have a positive impact on them. Using this story arc or plot diagram gives you the opportunity to have plenty of time to introduce different elements of the story and explain them in enough detail that your reader has time to collect all of the information they need to experience the story in a powerful manner.

Examples of Plot Outlines

There are many examples of plot outlines available to you, especially if you are an avid reader, television or movie watcher, or story listener. Virtually every story you have ever heard follows this structure in one way or another. However, to give you a few easy ideas of how this outline looks when it is in practice, let's look at two unique stories: The Three Little Pigs and Cinderella.

In three little pigs, we are introduced through the exposition where the three pigs are moving away from their family home, and each is in search of a new home. We are presented with who they are, what they are doing, and why. We are also given an idea of what is at stake for them: their homes. It moves forward into the rising action when we learn about each of the pigs looking for building materials and then building their homes. We learn that one builds theirs out of a weaker material (straw), one builds theirs out of a stronger material (twigs), and one builds theirs out of the strongest material (bricks). We are informed about the varying strengths of these materials, giving us the idea that there is some importance behind this piece of information but not yet introducing why. The story continues to rise as we later are introduced to the big bad wolf who comes along and huffs and puffs to blow down the first house which is made of straw. As you likely already know, the house blows down right away, and the pig runs off to his brother's house, which is made of twigs. The big bad wolf then goes and blows down the twig house and huffs and puffs and blows down that house as well. So, the two pigs are left running away to their other brother's house, which is made of bricks. There, the pigs are safe from the big bad wolf's huffing and puffing. The climax of the story arrives when the wolf finds a way to climb onto the roof of the house and comes down the chimney. There, he falls into a pot of boiling water, and the pigs cook him up. The falling action is that the pigs enjoy a feast together and are free of their fear of being eaten up by the big bad wolf. The resolution is that the three pigs end up sharing the home together and living with each other "happily ever after."

Cinderella is another popular fairy tale which also introduces us to what a plot diagram looks like in action. Here, the exposition lies within' Cinderella being introduced to the readers. We learn that she is a step-child and that her dad is no longer around, so she lives with her evil step-mom and two evil step-sisters. The step-mom and step-sisters live selfish lives of happiness and joy whilst forcing Cinderella to take care of the household by overseeing the chores and ensuring that it is well looked after. The rising action is when Cinderella overhears about an upcoming ball and insists that she wants to go. The step-mom says she can only go if all of her work is complete, and then ensures that there is so much work to be done that Cinderella will never be done in time. A fairy godmother comes and grants Cinderella her wish of going to the ball. She even ensures that Cinderella has a beautiful outfit and that she is cleaned up nicely for the experience so that she isn't late and all she has to do is get there. The climax arrives when Cinderella is at the ball. There, the prince falls in love with her and insists that they get married. When she realizes that the clock is about to strike midnight, she runs out without leaving her name or any contact information with the prince. However, she does lose a glass slipper on her way out of the ball. The falling action starts when the prince picks up the shoe and insists that he and his servants find Cinderella. They take the glass slipper and visit every house in the land to find the lady whom the glass slipper belongs to. Cinderella is almost robbed of the opportunity to try on the glass slipper when her step-mother tries to lock her in the basement, but she manages to get out. The resolution is finally granted to us when we learn that the glass slipper fits her perfectly and she is, in fact, the lady that the prince wanted to marry the night before. The step-mom is furious and so are the step-sisters as they learn that they are not the one who gets to marry the prince. Cinderella, on the other hand, is granted the opportunity to marry the prince, and she is freed from her life as a servant for her ungrateful and evil step-mom and step-sisters.

As you can see in both of these stories, there are very clear expositions, rising actions, climaxes, falling actions, and resolutions. These are the primary requirements of a story to keep it moving so that readers remain engaged and curious about how the story ends. Without these primary elements, the story may become stagnant, fail to draw readers through a chronological series of events that flow effectively through the storyline or otherwise deliver the story in such a way that helps us stay invested in it and curious as to what the resolution will be. Ultimately, the entire purpose of these plot diagrams is to ensure that your reader stays engaged with what the outcome will be, as you can see with these two examples.

Chapter 2: Building Your Plot

Now that you are aware of how a plot should look, it is time to begin building your own! In this chapter, we are going to explore the various steps of building your own plot line. You will be given all of the information you need to move from start to finish effectively. Even if you are not already aware of what your story is going to be, you will be given the opportunity to generate an idea within' this chapter. This chapter is all about helping you come up with a great idea and transform it into a powerful plot line that will help you generate a moving and engaging story that keeps your readers invested until the very end.

Step One: Get Inspired

The first part of writing a plot for your story is to get inspired. If you haven't already got an idea of what you want your story to be about, look for inspiration to help you pick a topic. You can find inspiration for stories in all areas of life from your day-to-day life to stories that other people tell you. You may even be able to reflect back on certain parts of your life or the life of someone you know and draw on experiences to help you become inspired on what you should write your book about. Alternatively, you may draw inspiration from other stories that you have heard or read. Ensure that when you are picking your story, however, that you don't directly copy someone else's story as this is a form of plagiarism. If you are drawing on inspiration from a story you've already heard or read before, take the time to look at the story from unique angles to see how you could write the same story only from a completely different perspective, potentially even with a different outcome altogether.

If you already have an idea of what you want to write your story about, take the time now to elaborate on that idea in your head. Look at it from all angles and see how you can ensure that you have a rich topic that will provide you with the opportunity to draw on it for plenty of material and substance to build your story from. You want to make sure that you have the entire idea of the story beforehand so that you have a general idea of where to go during the writing process. While you can certainly go ahead without a general idea, you will be losing all purposes of writing a plot line. And, ultimately, you will end up writing a story with no sense of direction that may result in you having a very bland, unexciting and otherwise boring story.

Step Two: Getting Direction

Now that you have generated your idea for what you want to write about, it is time to give yourself a sense of direction. This will ensure that you are clear on the focus of your story so that you can remain focused during the writing process. Creating a sense of direction for your story is extremely simple. Once you have generated the entire idea of what you want your story to be about, simply sum it all up into one sentence. Being able to sum it up in a single sentence means that you have clarity on what your story is and you are also clear on what the outcome will be. The outcome is ultimately what you need to know to have a sense of direction as this is what you are going to be writing toward. Below are a few examples of sentences that identify the entire plot of a story in a few words.

"An estranged sister returns to her brother's life so she can take his money and buy her way out of a dangerous situation."

"A bartender falls deeper in love with a regular patron each time he visits her bar and eventually they fall in love, get married, and buy the bar."

"A surgeon who is murdered by his patient that is a victim of neurotic episodes was believed to be a tragic victim, but later they discover that he was actually holding some very sensitive information that ultimately got him killed."

As you can see, each of these sentences gives a very direct insight as to what the story is going to be about and who is involved. It shows you who the protagonists are and what the outcome is for each of them. By identifying what the outcome is and whom it belongs to help give you, the writer, a sense of direction in regards to where you are going with your story. This sense of direction is what you want to keep in mind during the entire writing process as all events, thoughts, conversations, and other actions should ultimately lead up to it.

Step Three: Turning Your Idea into a Story

Once you have an idea and a sense of direction, it is time to turn your idea into a story. A great way to work with this part of the process is to start with the very basics and then build from there. That being said, start by writing down what you already know about your story. Anything you have already planned, brainstorm it on a piece of paper. Next, turn this brainstorm into some basic plot points. Be sure to add some twists, turns, unexpected events, wins, and losses along the way. Then, when you have completed that, take another piece of paper and write these points out along a plot line. If you are using lined paper, leave a few lines between each point. Don't worry about how you are going to organize these onto the story arc, they don't need to be in chronological form just yet. Instead, focus on getting them written down. Once you have, then you can start elaborating on the details of each of these points. Consider how each plot point contributes to the greater story and what should be involved so that it can contribute in a strong way. The best way to look at it is to view these unique plot points as tools. Each one will be used to drive your story forward and tell a certain part of it. You want to ensure that these tools are equipped with all of the pieces that they will need to provide a strong driving factor for your story. You don't necessarily need to know all of the factors of the story, but you should be taking the time to learn as much as possible. Ideally, you want to have at least 4-6 sentences about each plot point where you identify as many details about that plot point as you can. Remember, they don't need to be in chronological order so simply make sure that you are writing down anything that comes to mind that would be important to the story itself. As you are writing, you may find that you are in need of additional plot points so be sure that you take the time to brainstorm these and elaborate on them as well. This will ensure that you have all of the substance you need to generate a strong plot for your story.

Step Four: Create Your Story Arc

Now, you want to begin creating your story arc. This is going to be the outline that was described in chapter one, with the exposition, rising action, climax, falling action, and resolution. You can write this in list form by identifying each element of the arc, or you can draw it out on a piece of paper so that you can plan out your plot as though you are creating a timeline for your novel. Each method works, and in fact, it may be beneficial for you to do both, starting with the list and then moving over to the diagram, if you feel that you do better with the opportunity to both plan it out on a list and then get an idea of the final effect on the diagram.

Creating your story arc this way is what will ultimately give you the opportunity to get an idea of how your story looks overall. For this part, you want to step back from your detailing and look at the greater picture. Here is where you are going to identify where each plot point fits on the diagram, and where it should be placed in relevance to the other events taking place. Before you get started with placing anything on your diagram, read steps six and seven as they will provide you with important information about how you can do this effectively.

Step Six: Start with The End

When it comes to creating your plot, you want to start with the end. Remember, this is the direction you are heading in, and this is where you want your story to end up. You should be able to get an idea of what your end is going to look like based on the focus sentence you generated in step two. Now, however, you want to elaborate on that. This is going to be the first official plot point you outline on your story arc. Fortunately, it is an easy one. This point lies at the end of the map, so you can place it at the very end of your story arc. Once you have, identify what needs to happen in order for you to know that the end has been reached. What that means is identify the conditions, the state of mind, and any other relevant information that will take place at the end of the book that will be an indicating factor to you that the story has matured and is now ready to be ended.

As you read in step five, it is not necessary for you to go into specific detail about this point altogether as this should have already happened in step three when you were describing and elaborating on each plot point. Instead, simply refer back to that brainstorm if you need more information about all of the details surrounding the ending of your story.

Step Seven: Organize Your Plot Points on the Story Arc

Once you have identified the end-point, you want to start organizing the remaining plot points along your story arc. Now, this is the part where you need to pay attention. Here is where you may choose to put less detail into it if you want, especially if there are certain elements that you simply don't know yet, but ultimately having this plan created in the way that we are about to explore is what will ensure that you are clear on the focus and direction of your book and what you need to do to arrive at the outcome.

You want to start by working backward along the plot points. Pay attention to what your end point is, and then write everything on the line going backward from there. Reverse engineering your plotline in this way will ensure that you cover all of the important plot factors and that everything happens chronologically *for* your outcome, rather than it randomly appearing out of nowhere. Doing this actively ensures that everything makes sense and that it is built in the most solid form possible. It also ensures that your plot contains all of the information that is needed, and that you can easily find where each plot point belongs based on what needs to happen *before* the last plot point in order for it to have even occurred in the first place. For example, in order for the bank robber to rob the bank, he must first plan the robbery, therefore placing the plan *before* the action. Use this frame of thinking for each of your plot points, and they will all fall together on the line effortlessly.

Step Eight: Tying it All Together

Once you have successfully identified all of the different plot points, step back and take a look at your overall story arc. Pay attention to the different points you have included, and where everything falls. If it is too crowded, you may consider eliminating some of the less important plot points from the story arc so that you are not going further than what actually is required for the story itself. Alternatively, if you notice anything is missing take this time to identify what it is and include it in your story arc. Once you have, review it one more time to make sure all of the elements fit on it well and that they are all contributing to the overall story itself.

Finally, the best way to bring it all together is to write a few sentences about your story arc. Essentially you want to give an overview of your story based strictly on each plot point you have added on the story arc. For example, "Angela is a barista who has been working for a local coffee shop for six years. She recently met a new friend, Sam, who has been getting her into a lot of trouble. Her boss was worried about her, but this only made Angela feel guilty. To avoid the guilt, she quit her job as a barista and pursued a job in a sketchy nightclub with Sam. This lead to the girls being taken advantage of by a patron of the club, which ultimately leads them to find themselves in a basement of an unknown building." You would carry on writing sentences that walk you through each plotline along the way as this helps you see the flow of how your story will go. Obviously, you want to go into much more detail when writing the story and actually bring the reader along with you. However, writing it in this way allows you to see everything and make sure it all works together well. It can also help you identify anywhere that your plot may need to be altered, reorganized, strengthened, or otherwise adjusted to benefit the overall story.

It is vital that you take the time to look over the entire plotline after it has been laid out because this is what will ensure that you have made the best one possible. Of course, your plotline doesn't need to be intensely elaborate and overdone, but having it clearly defined and knowing the important details of each plot point will ensure that you have plenty to write about. It also helps ensure that you are clear on the direction of your story and that you don't end up going off track somewhere during the writing process. Furthermore, if you find that you are feeling stuck from an episode of writer's block, you can consult your plot line to help you move forward and stay on track with your writing.

Creating your plotline can take anywhere from a few hours to a few days. It all depends on how much time you are willing to invest in the process and how much you already know, or don't know, about your story. For some people, getting the inspiration for the story itself can take a few days or even weeks. Don't be discouraged if you find that this isn't a quick one-afternoon job for you. The best stories take time to accumulate, and they are well-planned in advance. The more prepared you are now, the stronger your story will be in the long run. While you don't need to plan so deeply that you take away any opportunity for you to be creative during the writing process, it certainly benefits to have clarity around your book, your goals, and what you envision the end result to be with your story.

Chapter 3: Bringing Your Plot to Life

Bringing your plot to life happens entirely through the writing process. However, there are many ways that you can ensure that you activate the right techniques during this process to really bring your plot to life. Ultimately, bringing your plot to life is the process of taking your story from being an outline on a page to being an actual book that moves your readers and keeps them engaged and invested in your book all the way until the end. In this chapter, we are going to identify important tips to consider when it comes to writing around your plot to ensure that it comes to life effectively for your reader.

Consider How Your Characters Fit In

Your characters are the voice to your story. They are also the tools you use to move your story from point to point. This makes them an extremely important element of your story overall. You will learn more about in-depth character development in the book "Character Development" of this series, but in the meantime, you should consider how they fit in overall. This is the part where you want to consider how each character is going to fit into the plot points, as well as how they will be affected by them. Primarily, you want to think about how each point will affect your protagonist and your antagonist. The more you are aware of how they are being affected, the easier it will be for you to write a compelling story that has your readers genuinely believing each point.

Since you haven't already established the in-depth portion of your characters, you should consider them in a general sense. For example, "In chapter six, Elise moves away which causes Jonathan to feel lost. Elise is affected by this move because she is moving away from her best friend and into a place where she doesn't know anyone. Jonathan is affected because he has a crush on Elise but he never managed to say anything before she left and now he doesn't think he will ever get the opportunity to tell her how she truly feels. He knows pursuing her dream career is good for her, but he can't help but feel a sense of guilt and hopelessness around the entire situation."

It is important that you consider your characters in each situation because this will help you get inside of their head more. This is important for character development, which you will learn about, but it is also important for story development. You want to make sure that the events move forward in a way that flows and is natural for the characters within' your story. If you are unsure about how to consider your characters in various plot points, use this generic question: "How does x affect y because of z?" For example, "How does moving affect Jonathan because of his love for Elise?" This question will help get you thinking about how each part of the book affects your characters and then plan out how you can use this in both the planning and writing processes.

Hide the Plot Effectively

When you are writing a plot, it is important that you learn to hide the plot effectively. Even though most readers are aware that there is a climax that typically involves some form of large conflict in virtually every book, it doesn't mean that they want to see the points of the plot sloppily put into every part of the book. Instead, they want to read the book and have that as a natural flow that is hidden in the background. Seamlessly hiding the plot within' your book requires a fair amount of practice, as well as a few techniques. One you will learn in the next section, which involves effectively transitioning between plot points. Another includes giving enough detail to each plot point within' the book that it is well discussed and does not feel as though it has been rushed through. Rushing through plot points detracts from the quality of your book and takes away from the reader experience by not giving them enough information about each plot point. You want to make sure that your reader understands why each element of the story exists and how it ultimately contributes to the story itself. It should feel as though the flow is moving naturally, not slow and not rushed.

Hiding the plot sequencing and story arc within' your story effectively means that your reader should not be able to easily identify when the next major story plot is coming, or what it will be. If you are not using a dynamic plot line and hiding it effectively, there is a good chance that your reader will be able to identify what your story is and determine the major plot points and outcome well before they ever got to those parts of the story. This takes away from the reading experience and generally leads to them putting the book down and not finishing it because they simply can't stay engaged. Effectively building and hiding your plotline avoids this.

Effective Transitioning Between Plot Points

It is important that you learn to effectively transition between plot points. If you are not highly practiced with this, you may want to identify what will take place during the transitions *before* you begin writing. These transition phases are heavily important to the story overall because they contribute to the natural flow of the story. Think about it, your life is not a series of major events. There are several things that take place in between the major things that happen in your life. The day-to-day events. While you don't want to bore your readers by repetitively sharing the same day over and over throughout the story, you also want to make sure that you give insight to your character's daily lives and what the calm is like between the storm. Take the time to naturally transition the plot along the major points, rather than simply jumping from one to the next. This is what gives your story a natural flow and prevents it from sounding stiff or uncomfortable.

There are many ways that you can transition between different plot elements, several of which will arise naturally as you are writing. However, the following points will give you some ideas as to how you can transition points if you are feeling stuck.

- Talk about day-to-day life, but switch it up with each transition that you use this strategy for. You may refer back to certain points, but don't explain the exact same events in great detail over and over. Instead, highlight different elements of the day-to-day experiences in between each transition.

- End the chapter and start the next one. While you don't want to use this strategy every time, it is a great way to start suspense. Make sure you don't jump right into the climax of the next plot point with the new chapter, but rather that you build up to it from a new angle than you would have with where you were previously. This also helps build suspense.

- Talk about the falling action from the previous plot point and then transition into the rising action of the next plot point.

You want to change up which strategy you use each time you are conducting a transition as using the same ones frequently can result in the book becoming predictable. While new chapters should bring new plot points, for example, they shouldn't happen at exactly the same time with the new chapter. You should not immediately feast into the rising action and place the climax of the new plot point within' the first page or two of the chapter. Instead, let the rising action linger, or even blend together two unique transition strategies for greater impact. The more you vary your approach and use unique angles, the better your overall story will be.

Have Action-Packed Plot Points

Plot points are meant to move the story forward, and while not all of them will be action-packed, you should certainly have a fair bit that it. Action-packed plot points encourage the reader to become further engaged in your book. They become interested in what is happening, how it ties into what has already happened, and what it could mean for the characters going forward. Effectively action-packed plot points littered throughout your story keeps it active and engaging for your readers, and it also helps move you forward toward the outcome. Action is where the motion is, so you want to use this tool as a strategy to help you move the story forward.

When you are using action-packed plot points, make sure you don't go too overboard. First, you want to have some of your plot points that are built differently, such as around emotional points. This will ensure that your reader doesn't become overwhelmed with action. Second, you want to make sure that the action makes sense to the story, that it moves the story forward, and that it doesn't overwhelm the reader. Using too much action can result in your reader feeling overwhelmed and struggling to keep up with your story. It also leads to them feeling disconnected from the story because they simply cannot relate to it; it doesn't seem like a realistic situation that would ever happen and therefore they are pulled out of the story.

Using action-packed plot points is a great tool that does not need to be used sparingly, but it does need to be used effectively. If you are interested in how you can add these to your story, consider looking at your overall plot and seeing where the action-based plot points are. Pay attention to what the action is, how it affects the story, and how you might be able to infuse more action into each plot point to get the most of it. However, make sure you keep a few that feature action but still have a more profound sense to them. These are the ones where something major happens, but it's not necessarily built around "and then, and then, and then." Instead, there is a large event that takes place which isn't clouded by several other events. This is a great way to make an event more profound, so if you need a certain plot point to carry a lot of meaning, make this one of the ones where there is less action built into it and more emotion built into it instead.

Make the Plot Engage the Reader's Emotions

In addition to having a plot that uses action to drive the story forward, have a plot that activates various emotions within' the reader to keep them engaged. Emotional attachment is what encourages a reader to stay connected to the story. When they develop a sense of attachment and concern for the protagonist, as well as some form of emotional resentment against the antagonist, readers are more likely to stay engaged in the book. Because they are genuinely invested in knowing how things turn out for the characters within' the book, they are more compelled to keep reading.

You can engage the reader's emotions in a variety of ways, but ultimately how you do so will be a part of your plot building. This is also a large part of what brings the plot to life for people. If they do not have a reason to care, they simply won't care. Instead, they will tune out. When you give people a reason to care, however, they are more interested, and therefore the entire story comes to life and fuels a passion within' them to carry forward. They feel empathy for your characters, and therefore you have the power to engage other emotions within' them to further draw them in and keep them moving forward.

The best way to engage emotions is to use the characters at each plot point to do so. For example, if someone dies in one of the plot points you can use the reactions of the characters to spark emotions such as relief, grief, anger, or otherwise. How you choose to spark emotions heavily relies on your decision, as well as where you want the story to go. This is all about the outcome, remember. You should seek to activate several of your reader's emotions throughout the duration of the story. While you don't want to infuse too many emotions into each situation, the story as a whole should dance on the emotional heartstrings of your readers in many different ways. The more emotional the experience is, the more enjoyable the read is.

Once again, you want to make sure that you are using emotions within' reason. You shouldn't be attempting to forcefully push your readers into extreme states of any given emotion. Instead, you want to suggest emotions through the actions, reactions, words, and thoughts of your characters and allow your reader to take it the extra mile on their own. Pushing it too hard can make it feel forced and unnatural, therefore taking away from the reading experience itself. You want the emotion to be believable, natural, and aligned with the story you are telling in each given moment throughout the book. When it comes to generating emotional reactions from your readers, you want to look at the book as a whole. See how you can use emotions overall, rather than how you can use them in each given moment. This will help you move your reader through emotions in a natural, well-developed way.

When it comes to infusing emotions, there is typically a certain way that emotions are infused into a plot line. In the beginning, readers are given opportunities to develop emotional attachments to the characters, so you want to emphasize on empathy in this part of the book. When you build empathy effectively here, you give your readers a reason to care for the rest of the book.

Next, you want to play on that empathy to generate a healthy connection between the characters and your reader as you are building the rising action in your plot line. Here, you want to use a lot of positive and happy emotions. You also want to use some feelings of sadness, grief, anxiety, anger, fear, and other emotions to help build up a sense of what the stakes mean for your character. These emotions also help build suspense and get your reader emotionally invested in the conflicts that are happening to your characters.

At the climax, you want to have a lot of energy built up. The specific emotion you emphasize on will depend on your unique genre. It may be love, anger, relief, resentment, frustration, fear, anxiety, or any other number of emotions depending on your genre and the story you are telling. This emotion is the one you want to charge the most as it is the highest point of your story. Therefore your reader really needs to *feel* like it is while they are reading.

As you move through the falling action, you want to highlight emotions like empathy, grief, sorrow, relief, and other emotions that you would typically feel after something major has finally happened. Again, the exact emotions you will use will be unique to your unique story. There are also a few important emotions you want to infuse into this part of your story. This part of your story should particularly focus on hope, faith, forgiveness, and rebuilding and moving forward with their lives. Since this is the path towards the resolution, you want them to genuinely feel that the resolution is coming and that the character feels hopeful for it, too. While they may lose hope sometimes, it should be a lingering emotion in the background.

When the novel ends, you typically want to give the reader a sense of closure. This is where you can give them the "happily ever after" that most readers come for. This could be a happily ever after where the characters truly achieved happier lives, or it could be one where they live the happiest version of their life that they possibly can based on the traumatic experiences that the characters recently endured. Once again, this will heavily depend on your story and the genre you are writing in. For example, romantic novels typically end in a feel-good happily ever after where the two lovers end up together and lead charmingly romantic lives until their old age. Alternatively, a mystery novel where someone is murdered in the beginning and the duration of the novel is spent discovering who did it should have a happily ever after whereby the murderer is found, the case is solved, justice is served, and the characters can move on with their healing process.

Chapter 4: Best Plot Building Advice

The basic plot-building advice and the eight-step process in chapter 2 give you a great foundation for creating your plot outline. However, you want to make sure that you take it that extra step further and have a great plot outline, and not just a "done" one. The following advice will help give you an insight as to how you can strengthen your plot and create a powerful one that will drive your story forward. These tips and tricks are provided from some of the best writers themselves, so you can trust that they are sound and will help you with building and troubleshooting your own plot!

Never Skip the Plot Building Process

The first tip you should know is that you never want to skip the plot building process. Even if you already know most of the information you want to share in your mind, you still want to build the plot. Building a plot allows you to get the information out of your mind and take it from a great plot to a phenomenal one. This process enables you to go deeper, question yourself and your intentions, and increase the quality of the plot overall. It also ensures that you can organize it and stay focused so that your story remains on track. It truly is essential in generating a well-structured, chronological and focused plot line that will drive your story forward and keep readers engaged.

Failing to create a plot line is truly a tragedy when it comes to your results. It often leads to the story lacking the depth that it could have, and ultimately not reaching its full potential. Because you didn't allow yourself to further explore your purpose, your plan, and your direction, you were never able to elaborate on it and strengthen it in a way that would serve your story even more than your initial idea already did. It can also lead to your story being sloppy, disorganized, and all over the place in such a way that your readers simply cannot follow, and therefore they fail to become engaged and stay invested in reading your book. If you want to have a book that makes sense, that engages your readers, and that has them craving more of your work, then you absolutely must start with a plot outline.

Build Strong Characters to Compliment Your Plot

Your plot is only as strong as your characters are. If you build a strong plot but fail to generate the right characters that can be used to drive the plot forward, you are not going to have a great story. Having a strong story that your readers will love ultimately comes from focusing on all elements of the story, including the plot. You should not primarily focus on the plot, the characters, the structure, or any other element of the story. Instead, you want to make sure that each individual part is well-developed so that they all work together like a well-oiled machine. Not only does this make the writing process easier, but it also maximizes the quality of your book and ensures that it reaches its fullest potential in all aspects.

Your characters are the ones that are involved in the plot, and they are the ones that you are speaking and acting through to drive it forward. If they are not developed enough, are not created specifically for the plot, or otherwise struggle to carry your plot forward, you are not going to have an incredible story. In fact, you may not even have a great one. Instead, you may have a mediocre one that was lost on characters who were not strong enough to carry the story forward. In the next book, you will learn about how you can develop your own characters, and you will also be walked through an in-depth character building exercise that allows you to generate the best possible characters. Ensure that you take the time to use that and build characters specifically for your story and plotline so that they carry it forward and lead you towards complete success with your book.

Have a Powerful Outcome

The outcome of your story is what it's all about. Literally, the entire story building up to that point is only there for that specific point. People want to know how things turn out for all of the characters involved so they remain invested until the end, curious about what the outcome will be. If your outcome is not powerful enough, your readers are going to be heavily disappointed. There are a few things to keep in mind when it comes to developing your outcome, which we will explore now.

First, you want to avoid your outcome being too "flat" for the story. It should be full of some form of emotion that leaves your reader genuinely feeling something when the book ends.

They should feel hopeful, grateful, happy, or otherwise positive about the ending of the story. Additionally, they should feel as though they have been granted with closure from the ending. Your reader should feel that all loose ends have been tied and that anything that was lingering in the story was explained before you drew the story to a close. They should be feeling satisfied and complete with the story you have provided, and not like they are left wondering about any other element. Unless, of course, you are purposefully ending on a cliffhanger to help draw them into the next book of a series, you want to avoid leaving your readers with a cliffhanger. Instead, you want to provide them with a sound ending that makes them feel happy for the character like their goal was achieved because they accomplished what they had set out to accomplish in the beginning when we were presented with the primary problem.

When you are generating your outcome, you also want to make sure that it leaves a powerful impact on your reader. This comes from the emotions, but it should come from the thoughts as well. A great way to do this is to leave them reflecting on a part of their own life, reflecting on the story itself, or even feeling as though they have learned a lesson through the reading process. The ending should be sort of like a grand finale for your reader, complete with a drum roll and fireworks.

Use a Natural Ending Point

To elaborate on how to end your story, you want to ensure that you choose a natural ending point. You do not want to pick a spot that feels unnatural like something has been left unsaid, or like the reader isn't getting the full gist of the story. You also don't want to carry on well after the natural ending point has come as this will dilute the quality of your ending. Instead, you want to make sure that you keep it powerful by providing plenty of information, but only the necessary information. It is important that you remember that the outcome is the part of the book that will remain freshest in your readers mind so this is the part that should have the biggest impact on them.

Let Your Characters Resolve Their Own Conflict

Many stories fall flat when they let a force of nature or some unknown hero come in and save their characters from the problems that have arisen throughout the story. In some cases, this helps. In the majority, however, it is a very weak technique that takes away from the story. Readers are drawn into a story because they develop a connection to the character. So, naturally, they want to watch the character develop and see the natural conflict resolution by the character. They want to know how this has changed them, how it has helped them grow, and what they have learned from it. Not only does this allow the reader to feel as though they are spying through a peephole into the life of the character, but when done properly it also helps the reader learn some things from the character, too. When readers feel connected to the character, it is often because they relate in some way. Therefore, when the character naturally evolves, it causes the reader to look within' themselves and see how they have grown, or how they might grow in the future as a result of what they have witnessed in your characters. For this to happen, however, there has to be a change in your character that takes place naturally. This means that it is important that you let your character resolve their own conflict. While you can allow heroes and random acts of nature take the credit on smaller subplots within' the story, it is important that the major changes and lessons are directly through the character themselves.

Be Original

If the story you are writing has already been written and you are only changing the names and a few basic points in the book, you are going to lose traction with readers. Books that are outstanding and that become known as great and even phenomenal books are ones that are written out of originality. Everything else gets tossed in the bargain bin within' a few days from their launch. You want to make sure that you are writing an original story that your reader will not feel like they have already read. If they feel like the story is too similar to another one they have read, then your story becomes both predictable and unexciting. You may even damage your writing reputation by essentially copying someone else's work. And, if you're not careful, you could infringe on plagiarism rules. It is important that you generate an original plot that your reader doesn't know from previous stories. While it will certainly share similarities to others in the genre and it may borrow some ideas or techniques from other books, the overall product should be unique and original from what has already been written and released. This will ensure that you keep your readers engaged and interested throughout the reading process and that your story has the potential to climb to best-seller rating, rather than simply be skimmed through and dropped just as quickly.

Use an Exciting Plot

Readers don't *want* to get engaged with your book, they *need* to. If you use a plot that lacks excitement, you are going to struggle to get your readers engaged, and therefore you will fail to meet their expectations and have them raving about your book. Instead, they will simply close the book and won't recommend it to anyone else. Or, worse, they will leave a negative review on reviewing platforms about your book, discouraging others from giving it a chance, too. What you need is an exciting plot that will keep your readers engaged and invested from the time they open the book until the time they finish reading it. Your readers should feel like they don't want to put the book down when they're reading it, and like they can't wait to get back to it once they have. They should be heavily invested in the characters, the stakes, the conflicts, and the story itself. Doing this requires you to have an exciting plot.

An exciting plot is one that moves forward. It should not go straight from point A to point B, though. Instead, it should take many unexpected twists, turns, and side steps as it advances towards the final outcome. The reader should not know what to expect, but they should be emotionally invested in each part of it. Every plot point that you include should contribute to the overall story in some way, even if the reader doesn't understand how right away, or until much later. The more effectively you keep the story exciting and interesting, the more you will generate raving readers who are eager to share your book with others and encourage them to give it a read themselves.

Switch Up the Pace

When it comes to writing a fiction novel, you always want to emphasize on how it compares to reality. Even if you are writing a fantasy novel, the pace at which the book moves should be comparable to reality itself. There should be parts where it is fast, and parts where it moves slower. There should be areas where strong emotions are sparked, and there should be areas where no emotions are sparked. Your reader should feel as though the book ebbs and flows, much like an ocean tide. This gives them the opportunity to move along with the story at a natural, realistic pace. During the times of action and emotion they are heavily engaged and are rapidly being fed new information, and during the times of calm and more relaxing emotions, they are given the opportunity to reflect on recent events while also seeing how the characters are doing the same. Switching up the pace gives your book a realistic flow that keeps readers believing it to be true and maintains their ability to relate to it in some way at most times.

Stay On Track

Subplots are a great way to add depth to your book. However, too many can result in your book going off track and becoming confusing to the reader. You should not be darting around with information, sharing too many subplots, or diving into information that is entirely irrelevant to the overall story. Instead, you want to make sure that you are staying focused on the end result. Any subplot that somehow contributes to the overall story by giving it depth, allowing you to further explain certain elements of people or the plot, or otherwise increasing the quality of your story should be considered. Those that add enough value that makes them worthwhile should be kept. All other subplots should be ignored. When it comes to staying focused, make sure that you never divulge into information that is entirely irrelevant to the story. Unless it is drawing the reader towards the outcome, teaching them more about your characters, or otherwise providing them with a value that contributes to the story itself, you should not be sharing it. Getting carried away with irrelevant information results in your reader becoming confused. It dilutes your story and makes your readers want to close the book because they simply don't grasp what you're trying to tell them.

Have A Strong "Why"

Your "why" is your outcome. It is the reason why you are writing the story. Are you writing it to teach people who murdered the person in the beginning? Are you writing it to share a romantic love story between two people? Are you doing it to dive deeper into a fantasy world that you have built in your imagination and to bring life to it? Are you doing it to teach your reader a lesson? Why are you writing your book? Knowing why the book is being written in the first place can help with a significant number of writing elements. Your why is ultimately what will help you generate your plot as it will ensure that you are creating plot points that are relevant to the overall story, or the "why." It also ensures that your story stays focused. Furthermore, it helps your readers feel the significance of your novel. Your "why" for writing it will also be their "why" for reading it. They need to feel the significance and impact of this so that they feel compelled to read your book in the first place and to continue reading it until it ends. This is how they will get the biggest impact from your book, so you want to make sure that you are clear as to why you are writing it in the first place.

Don't Abuse Writing Techniques

Writing techniques are like tools that you use to structure your story, create certain causes and effects, and ultimately design your entire story in a way that impacts the reader the way the story is intended to. They are an incredible selection of tools that you absolutely need to use to generate a phenomenal story that your readers will love. However, you have to be aware when using these techniques. You never want to abuse them by overusing them, using them in the wrong area, or otherwise misusing them. When they are not used properly, these techniques take away from the story, and you dilute their impact overall. It is important that you use the right techniques in the right places and that you don't overuse them so as to eliminate the effect they have on your story.

Learn as You Go

One of the best pieces of advice that can be given is to learn as you go. Don't be afraid to make mistakes, take on criticism, and increase your skill by actively practicing it. Remember, you can't learn something if you don't practice in the first place. You don't try something and become an overnight master with it. You have to use the skill, practice the skill, and expand on the skill as regularly as possible if you are going to become a master at it. The best writers got to where they are today by practicing, listening to feedback, and improving their own skills. One great way to go about it is to keep a notebook and write down feedback you get, as well as ideas or thoughts you have along the way. This gives you something solid to look back on and reflect on when it comes to increasing your skill and doing better in the future.

Conclusion

Thank you for reading *"Plot Writing: Step-by-Step | Essential Story Plotting, Conflict Writing and Plotline Tricks Any Writer Can Learn"*. This book was designed to help you take your plot deeper, increase your writing skills, and give your story a greater sense of purpose to keep your reader engaged and entertained along the way.

I hope this book was able to provide you with new, revolutionary, and insightful tips and tricks to help you with your plot. I also hope that you were able to use the eight-step plot building guide to help you generate a plot that will powerfully drive your story so that you can create the next best-seller. Remember, these tips are ones that can take you to the next level, but it is up to you to implement and practice them if you are going to take it all the way. Only you have the power to materialize the stories in your head and share them with the world! Practicing will help you do this with maximum impact.

The next step is to create your own plot line that will enrich your story and carry it to the end. Remember, reverse engineering is the best way to ensure that your story features everything it requires, so always look at things backward, if not starting backwards to begin with. Additionally, make sure that you take the time to read the next book where you will learn to develop incredible characters that will compliment your plot perfectly and help you take your book to the top. Recall that a book is like a well-oiled machine whereby all of the elements such as the structure, plot line, outline, and characters are built together to operate seamlessly and create a relatable, realistic story that your readers will love. Each element should be individually developed with the intention of it being a part of the greater story so that they contribute to the greatness of your novel.

Thank you, and good luck!

CHARACTER DEVELOPMENT

STEP-BY-STEP

ESSENTIAL STORY CHARACTER CREATION, CHARACTER EXPRESSION AND CHARACTER BUILDING TRICKS ANY WRITER CAN LEARN

SANDY MARSH

BOOK 6: CHARACTER DEVELOPMENT

STEP-BY-STEP

Essential Story Character Creation, Character Expression and Character Building Tricks Any Writer Can Learn

Sandy Marsh

reparation, damages, or monetary loss due to the information herein, either directly or indirectly.

Respective authors own all copyrights not held by the publisher.

The information herein is offered for informational purposes solely, and is universal as so. The presentation of the information is without contract or any type of guarantee assurance.

The trademarks that are used are without any consent, and the publication of the trademark is without permission or backing by the trademark owner. All trademarks and brands within this book are for clarifying purposes only and are the owned by the owners themselves, not affiliated with this document.

Table of Contents

Introduction

Thank you and congratulations for purchasing *"Character Development: Step-by-Step | Essential Story Character Creation, Character Expression and Character Building Tricks Any Writer Can Learn"*.

This book will help you with every aspect of character building, from creating the basic structure for your character to designing their personality and even helping develop them alongside the development of your story. Everything you will learn within' this book will ensure that you are equipped with all of the knowledge you need in order to create characters that are compelling and that your readers can fall in love with.

If you have read the previous five books from this series, then you will know just how important your characters are to your story. This guidebook will provide you with all of the knowledge you need in order to help create strong characters that will move your story forward and assist you in building the powerful and important emotional attachment between your reader and your characters.

Each chapter within' this book will provide you with part of the character building process. Within' that part you will be given step-by-step instructions so that you can easily create the best characters possible, knowing that they have been designed with every necessary feature to make them powerful additions and tools for your storytelling process. Without further ado, feel free to dive on into the character building experience. Enjoy!

Chapter 1: The Basics

It is no secret how important characters are to your story. They are the individuals that the story is about. Therefore, they are responsible for the story itself. They help you create the story, move the story forward, and introduce change and other action along the way. Without characters, there would be virtually no way for you to design a story.

Before we explore how you can build your own characters, we are going to explore the basics and important features of characters. This will help you understand more about why characters are so important and why you need them. It will also give you a foundational understanding of each unique style of character and how they can serve your story overall.

Why Characters Are Important

Stories are essentially created through verbal or written recollections of events that took place. In literary work, thoughts, choices, words, consequences, and actions are all important elements that are responsible for contributing to the plot line. Naturally, these qualities must be expressed in some form or manner. Since these are human qualities, it makes sense then that they would be expressed through a human-based character. Alternatively, such as in children's stories, they may be expressed through animal characters that possess these human-like qualities.

Characters are an important tool used by authors and writers to move stories forward. These are the personalities that give them the power to add the element of thought, action, words, choices, and consequences into their book. Without characters, they would essentially be describing a scene whereby nothing would be happening because there would be no one for it to happen to, for, or as a result of.

In order to establish themselves as useful tools that are used to move a plot forward, characters can be broken down into twelve categories. You will learn more about each of these categories in the next section. However, it is important to understand that each of these categories was designed to help create powerful and useable tools that writers can call on to help them progress the story forward.

Types of Characters

When you read a novel, you may be surprised to know that characters go a lot deeper than you think. In the novel, you watch the characters evolve, and new ones come and go along the way, but you may not understand how much actually goes into the development of these characters. When authors want to create a story that has a great deal of depth and can easily be believed as a real-life person, it is important that they understand the different types of characters that exist and how they can serve their story.

Naturally, fiction characters are made up. While they may be completely based on real people or have certain features borrowed from people that the author knows in real life, they are still made up characters. This is how the author is able to use them to build and move the story along because the characters can be used to achieve any outcome the author desires to create.

The following character styles will introduce you to twelve different types of characters that exist within' stories. By understanding each unique type of character, you can see how they can serve your story. Furthermore, you can decide what style each character will be designed in which will make it easier for you to discover the guidelines for creating the said character in the long run.

Major or Central Characters are characters that the story revolves around. These are the primary characters within' the story, and they are crucial to the development of the story itself. These are the characters who are presented with conflicts and who are responsible for executing the resolutions. Almost every part of the entire novel will revolve around these particular characters. They are often the main character, as well as that character's friends and family, or coworkers, or anyone else who will be used as a recurring character within' the story. These are some of the most important characters within' your novel because without them you will not have a story to tell. You want to emphasize your development on these characters to make sure that they are realistic, believable, and relatable to your readers.

Minor Characters are characters that are used to serve the major and central characters. These characters have a powerful role in helping to move the plot forward and often have as much depth as the major characters do. They are only considered minor characters, however, because they don't tend to recur as frequently as the major characters will and they are not a part of the central story. For example, they may be a sister that lives on another continent but comes to visit for a short time or even a few times for the duration of the novel. Alternatively, it may be a few coworkers that recur here and there but are not a part of the central theme or the majority of the major plot points. These are important characters because they help provide realistic depth to the book by broadening the scope of characters without taking complete attention away from the major characters themselves.

Dynamic Characters is a phrase used to represent characters that change over the course of the novel. Virtually anyone who changes his or her personality, belief system, morals or values, or even simply matures over the course of the novel is considered a dynamic character. These characters typically evolve for reasons primarily relating to the central theme of the book, such as the central conflict or a major crisis that they face that ultimately contributes to the books overall theme. Dynamic characters are not necessarily any one group of characters themselves. However, they can be virtually any character within' the book. The majority of the dynamic characters in a novel will typically be the major characters because these are the ones that are directly moving the story forward through change, as you learned about in previous books within' this book series. They may also turn out to be any other character within' the book, however. So long as a character changes in some noticeable way from the beginning to the end of the book they are considered a dynamic character.

Static Characters are the exact opposite of dynamic characters. These ones do not change over the course of the story. Instead, they remain the same. Completely unchanged. Static characters are not suitable to be major characters because they do not help progress a story or serve in the way of creating change in any way, shape, or form. Instead, static characters are usually minor characters. These characters still provide the author with the opportunity to use them as tools to spark change in the main characters, but they are not always required to change in order for the successful progression of the story.

Round Characters are unlike dynamic characters and unlike static characters altogether. These characters are ones that feature highly complex personalities. They may experience frequent conflicts, or they may even contradict themselves on a regular basis. These characters are also rarely used as major characters because the required personality type does not serve as a powerful foundation to generate a dynamic and moving character.

Flat Characters, unlike rounded characters, flat characters are typically notable for one single personality trait. This characteristic is one that should be the primary defining factor, influence, and expression that is used by the character. When you are creating a flat character, they are often much like a static character. And, similar to static characters, they are not suitable for the central characters because this personality does not provide the author with the opportunity to generate a moving enough character that will lead someone through a plot line.

Stock Characters are considered to be stereotypical characters that are almost expected in certain stories. For example, a cynical but moral private eye, mad scientists, and faithful sidekicks are all stock characters. These are all people that you would expect to be present in certain books. They generate the name "stock character" because of repetitive use in certain story types and structures. These characters typically have flat personalities, but may also have rounded personalities in some cases. They are a great element to add to your story because they give the reader something that they can identify with and expect, as well as someone that helps them feel like they can better relate to the story. It is a great way to give your reader a point to engage with through providing them with a familiar presence.

Protagonist is the word used to describe the central character in your story. This is the primary character that the story follows. They are at the center of your central characters, and they provide the main storyline. Most people call this the "main character," and they are identified as the "most important role in the story" to most, although this is not entirely true. Although this person is the reason the story exists, they are not the only one responsible for moving the plot forward. Therefore they are not the most important role. Still, they are highly important. This character should be dynamic and well-developed, as this will be the one your reader is going to follow most. Although the protagonist may not be the most likable character, they are the one that should be used in order to command that the reader experiences emotions, particularly empathy, for them. This way they can be used to draw the story forward and keep the reader engaged along the way.

Antagonist is the word used to describe either a character or a situation that operates against the protagonist. This is the opposition and the oppressive force that is trying to stop or otherwise hinder the success of the protagonist. This is the obstacle the protagonist faces that they must find the strength, knowledge, and power to overcome if they are going to generate a successful happy-ending story. As mentioned in the beginning, the antagonist can be a character *or* a situation. It can also be both. Even if you are using a situation instead of a character for your antagonistic force, you still want to go through the effort of making it well-developed so that the reader can believe it and understand why it is such a threat to the protagonist and their stakes.

Anti-Hero is a word used to describe a character that presents itself in certain stories. This is usually the protagonist, and they are called the anti-hero because they possess many features that make them unlikeable. They may have questionable morals, negative behavioral traits, or other characteristics that are not typically admired by the average person. This person may be the kind of individual that your reader would never want to associate with or root for, but still, they are the center of the story, and they find themselves following them and feeling empathy for this character when certain events happen. Writing an anti-hero protagonist can be difficult, but if you can master it, it is a great practice to help you increase your ability to generate empathy and emotional attachments between readers and your characters.

Foil Characters are those who have personalities and characteristics that often clash with other central characters in the novel. These characters may be used to represent the antagonist or a supporting character. They are designed by creating a character who has qualities that contrast the protagonist's character, or another important character within' the storyline. This contrast may seem unimportant, but from a writer's perspective, it provides you with the opportunity to highlight certain characteristics about your protagonist or other central character by emphasizing the differences between them and the foil character.

Symbolic Characters are ones that are used to resemble major parts of society through one character. These characters may be any major or minor character within' your story, so long as the entire purpose of the character is to highlight a certain aspect of society through their actions, beliefs, and values.

How Characters Are Presented and Revealed

Presenting and revealing characters is your opportunity to teach your reader who the character is and what they're all about. This is where you get the ability to introduce them to different characteristics and traits that the reader should know about the character, and how these traits contribute to the way that the character ties into the storyline.

There are only two ways that you can present your characters to your readers: either through direct or indirect presentation.

Direct presentation is the method you use when you are directly telling your readers about who the character is. For example, if you were to write "Presenting to you, Christopher Adams, a self-righteous, ignorant, and exploitative agent who preys on his clients for their money." In this circumstance, you are directly telling your reader who Christopher Adams is and what his most outstanding traits are. You can also do it in a more positive light, such as "Meet Mary Willows, a school teacher who spends her time eating peanut butter sandwiches and teaching preschoolers how to count to five. She is always bright and cheery, and will put a smile on your face faster than even a puppy could." In essence, direct presentation is described as any type of presentation you make whereby you tell the reader what they need to know.

Indirection Presentation is naturally the exact opposite of direct presentation. This is the tactic you use when you leave it up to the reader to get to know a character through his or her words, thoughts, and actions. They get to know this person through what they say and do throughout the book, allowing them to generate their own theories on who this character is. Still, you use their words and actions to help you create the overall illusion as to what makes the character who they are. This form of presentation is very similar to the natural way that we get to know people since we are not given direct answers when we meet people.

Instead, we have to learn about them based on what they say and do. Unlike direct presentation, indirect presentation is the tactic used when authors allow readers to formulate judgments and opinions on characters without ever telling them about the quality traits these characters have. Sometimes the reader will know exactly who the character is and their judgment is right, and other times they will be proven wrong over the course of the book.

To make it easier for you to use these two presentation methods to introduce who your characters are, we have compiled a list of the eleven basic ways that you can present your characters to your readers. This list is compiled to provide examples of both direct and indirect presentation methods. You can also use it as a test to see if you can determine which would be considered direct and which would be considered indirect so that you can better understand how both of these presentation styles work.

1. Present your character by having them say things in a particular way.

2. Present your character by having them say certain things.

3. Present your character by providing insight into their environment.

4. Present your character by exploring what they think.

5. Present your character by providing a physical description of them.

6. Present your character by providing a psychological description of them.

7. Present your character by telling readers what other people say or think about them.

8. Present your character by having them do certain things.

9. Present your character by having them do things in a particular way.

10. Present your character by the way that they react to other's actions and words.

11. Present your character by the way that they react to their own actions and words.

Chapter 2: What Makes a Character Great

Since you are researching how to make the characters for your novel, let's assume that you don't just want to make a good character. Instead, you want to make a great character. You want to make the kind of character that people are eager to read more about. This character is one that the reader can somehow attach to. It also gives you the best tool to help you move your story forward, regardless of what type of character you are creating. Some of these techniques should be used on all characters while others only need to be used on a few, which you will learn about as you read on. Still, every character in your novel is important to the storyline itself. Therefore, they all need to be great characters. This chapter will help you identify exactly what is required in order for you to be able to do just that.

Have Characters that Are Likeable

While not all of your characters have to be likable, many should be. Your protagonist, for example, should be a likable character unless you are spinning them off as an anti-hero. Having likable characters in your book will make people have an easier ability to emotionally connect to your characters. Just as you would prefer to spend time with and invest your energy in people you like in real life when people read they also like to invest their energy and attention into characters that they like. At least a few of your characters should be likable so that your reader feels as though they can relate to the character and generate some form of emotional attachment and relationship with that character as they read your story.

As you are creating likable characters, however, avoid making them saint-like. You do not want to have a character that is *too* likable or features little to no flaws because this actually goes back in the opposite direction. It takes away from the realistic values of your character and makes them seem unapproachable, which, ironically makes them unlikeable. So, avoid trying to make your characters *too* likable, or people won't like them! Instead, create a realistic character who has believable flaws that are enough to balance out their likable qualities so that they are still likeable while also being realistic and relatable.

Have Characters that Are Not Likeable

In addition to having characters that are likable, you need to have ones that aren't! Any real-life story would include people who are not liked by the protagonist, and who may be unlikeable in general. These are the ones whose flaws outweigh their good traits. They are still human, therefore they still naturally have some good qualities to them, but overall they are not likable as a person. In a typical story, this is your antagonist, but it doesn't always have to be. Furthermore, you can have more people who are unlikeable, such as someone who is related to or close to the protagonist. Using unlikeable characters helps to balance out the number of likable characters you have, thus making the story sound more relatable and realistic.

Again, you don't want to create a character that is *too* unlikeable, or people aren't going to believe it. Typically, even the worst people have some positive characteristics to them that make them worth having empathy for, even if we don't tend to like them in general. Make sure that you keep your unlikeable character's human by giving them some characteristics that make them seem as though they *could* be likable in some way or another, even if only a little.

Make Your Characters Good at What They Do

Even though your characters, particularly your protagonist, should face difficulties and come to the end of their rope once or twice before finally succeeding, they should still succeed in the end. Furthermore, they should be good at what they do, even if it isn't always enough to get them to a full success. For example, they should be a phenomenal secret agent that is exposed to acts of god that make it impossible for them to capture the bad guy until *finally* things go right and they succeed at last. Even if they make mistakes from time to time or they struggle to be the best here and there, they should typically be good at what they do. If they aren't, people are going to wonder why they are even trying to begin with and it will make the story unlikeable.

Think about stories such as the James Bond ones. If James Bond were to fail every mission he ever set out to accomplish it would not make for a good story. People may laugh their way through one show, but it would not last, and they certainly wouldn't have many different movies based on this hero. Likewise, your heroic character should be good at what they do, and they should be worthy of your reader cheering them on for the duration of your story.

Give Your Characters a Strong Charisma

Having characters that are charismatic increases their likeability. It doesn't only draw in other characters, but it draws in the reader as well. While charisma as far as good looks can be a beneficial factor, this is more about their qualities. Make them someone who lights up the room when they walk in it. Maybe they are particularly happy, or they always have a good joke to share. Or, maybe they are great at complimenting others and making them feel good about themselves. Whatever way you choose to build charisma in the character, make sure you take the time to actually establish it. Remember, you want likable characters and charisma is one great way to create a character that can be liked. The more drawn into the character your reader is, the more invested they will become in your story overall.

Have Dynamic Characters

Characters that love to take driven action and grow alongside your plot line are great when it comes to building a strong book. As you know, it is good to have your protagonist as a dynamic character. However, you should consider adding a few other dynamic characters as well. Having the antagonistic character, as well as supporters of both the protagonist and antagonist being designed to be dynamic characters means that you have plenty of opportunities to pursue action in your story. It also makes the story much more relatable and realistic.

When you are creating dynamic characters, know that not every character in the story needs to be dynamic. In fact, it is better to have a strong balance between dynamic and static characters. Remember, in real life, we have a little bit of everything. If you can look at your own life, there are likely people who have never changed or haven't been in your own life story enough for their change to be recognized, and then there are those who have grown drastically since you met them. Just like in real life, your book needs to have a healthy mixture of both as well. This will ensure that your reader feels as though your story is compelling and enjoyable.

Let Your Characters Suffer

Some of the novels are going to require your characters to suffer. Conflicts, complex issues, and various situations would lead to any normal person facing the experience of suffering in their own life. The same goes for your characters. If someone dies, let the character suffer. Allow them to feel the suffering. If they lose something, something doesn't go their way, or they are otherwise facing challenges, allow them to experience some suffering alongside those challenges. This makes them more believable and relatable. Furthermore, it draws your reader's emotions into the story even more. Letting your character suffer somewhat is a great way to build empathy from your reader to your character. Once your reader has empathy, they are much more likely to care about what's next for your character. They want to see the character do well and they are eager to see them win, so the reader roots even more for your character. You can build on this throughout the story by introducing a few different instances of suffering. Just, as with everything, make sure you don't go overboard and have too much suffering, or the book will be too depressing and unbelievable to read!

Know Your Character Intimately

It is important that you know your character intimately. Even more intimately than your readers ever will, even though they need to get to know them intimately as well. When you know your characters intimately, you can easily talk about them, share their story, and give insight into their inner world. This is because you would know how they would think, speak, act, and react in various situations. You also know their preferences, dislikes, likes, and other important characteristics about them.

Think about someone that you know well. You have likely known someone at one point or another in your life so well that you know exactly what they would do or say in most situations. This is how intimately you need to know your characters, as this is the intimacy that will allow you to write about them in any and every situation that will arise throughout your novel. You should know exactly how that person would respond to everything you throw their way so that you can create a realistic and believable character. This is what takes your character from a profile on paper to a real person in your fiction novel.

Chapter 3: Character Building Step-by-Step

Now that you are clear on why characters are important, the basics about characters, and what makes a character great instead of just good, you are ready to start actually building your characters. As you go through this chapter, keep what you have already learned in mind as it will help you stay focused and create successful characters along the way.

In this chapter, you are going to discover step-by-step guidance for picking whom you want to cast in your book, as well as how you can develop each character so that they serve your book in a powerful and profound way. Depending on what type of character you are working towards developing, you will discover a guide to help you develop that kind of character. This will ensure that each character is developed enough to be useful in your novel, but that you aren't wasting your time over-developing characters that do not require it, such as minor static characters.

Choosing Your Cast

Before you begin developing your characters you need to decide which characters you want to cast in your book. That is, you need to decide how many characters you are going to need to actually write the book. While you may find that some additional ones come up or you feel naturally called to pull in new characters along the way, you should start out with a pretty strong idea as to whom your central, minor, and other characters are going to be from the beginning. Anyone who is going to be essential to your central story should be outlined and developed before you begin writing. This will ensure that you know exactly how and when to present them, and their presentation is natural and strong based on their unique character and role in the novel.

The best way to choose how many characters you need for your novel is to refer back to your story structure and outline. Looking at your story structure and outline will give you the opportunity to consider each major plot point. As you do, consider which characters should be present for the plot point, as well as which ones are necessary for it. Take your time and work your way through the plot, picking out characters as you go. Once you have, take a look at the "in between" parts, too. For example, in between major plot points, you may need additional characters to keep the story flowing, such as people in line at a bank or the cashier at the local grocer. This is the best way to determine what characters you need in your novel and will have you well on your way to a strong character roster.

Once you have determined which characters are needed for the plot, you want to get more specific about them. First, make sure that you haven't picked too many characters. A book with too many characters can be overwhelming and can lead to your reader forgetting who is who. However, you want to make sure that you have enough that you can make it feel like real life. The best way to make sure you have enough characters, and not too few or too many, is to make sure that every single character you choose to create is essential to the story itself. Then, you need to decide what kind of character they're going to be. Are they going to be a major character or a minor character? Additionally, will they be round, flat, static, or dynamic? Pay attention to these features as they will help you determine how to create them.

Creating Your Characters

Central characters are the main characters in your novel. They include the protagonist, the antagonist, and any other characters that are regularly involved in the plot, including major plot scenes. When you are creating central characters, you want to go heavily into depth about who they are and why they are that way. Below you will find several categories filled with questions. Answering these questions will help you answer about who your character is, which will help you develop them and learn a great deal of information about them. This way you can get to know them intimately and write about them effortlessly.

Character's General Information

1. What is your character's name?

2. Do they have a nickname? If so, what is the story behind it and who gave it to them?

3. Do they like their nickname?

4. What is their birthday?

5. Where were they born?

6. What ethnicity are they?

7. Do they have any religious views?

8. Do they practice their religion?

9. Where do they currently live? (Be specific with their address)

10. Do they rent the place or own it?

11. Briefly describe their home.

12. Does anyone else live with them?

13. What is it like where they live? (i.e., city, town, etc.)

14. Do they like living here? If not, why not? Where would they rather be?

15. What type of home décor do they have? (i.e., expensive, neat, inexpensive, comfortable, etc.)

16. What is the first impression someone would have to their home?

17. Do they have pets? If not, why not? If they do, what kind, what are their names, and how many? How do they treat their pets?

18. What job do they presently have, how long have they had it for, and where is their job located?

19. Do they like their job?

20. How much money do they make?

21. What educational background do they have?

22. Do they drive? If so, what kind of vehicle do they have? Be specific.

23. What is their sexuality?

24. Are they in a romantic relationship with anyone? If so, who and for how long?

25. Do they have any previous romantic partners that are significant to the story?

26. What do they call their current spouse? (i.e., nicknames)

27. How did they meet their spouse?

28. Do they have any children? Give specific details if they do. (i.e., age, birthday, gender, name, who the parents are, etc.)

29. If they have children, describe the relationship they share with each child.

Physical Appearance

1. How tall is this character?

2. What do they weigh?

3. What body type do they have? (i.e., skinny, curvy, overweight, athletic, etc.)

4. What color are their eyes?

5. Do they use glasses, contacts, or hearing aids? Or any other medical devices?

6. What is their skin tone?

7. Do they have any prominent features that one might notice about them? (i.e., freckles, birthmark, scar, tattoos, etc.)

8. What is their face shape?

9. Whom do they look similar to?

10. What is their overall health like?

11. Do they have any chronic illnesses or conditions?

12. Are there any current health problems they are facing?

13. How do they dress? (Including cost range of clothes and specific style)

14. Do they dress to be noticed, or just to be dressed?

15. Do they wear any special or significant pieces of jewelry or accessories?

16. How does this character approach their grooming habits? (i.e., extremely neat, unkempt, etc.) Why do they groom themselves this way?

17. What hairstyle does this character have?

18. What is the natural hair texture for this character?

19. If they typically groom their hair for a different texture, what is it?

20. What is their natural hair color?

21. If they dye their hair, what color is it now?

Communication

1. When communicating, what is the pace that this person communicates with? (i.e., fast, slow, average)

2. What tone of voice do they have?

3. Do they have any words they tend to use or favor in general conversation?

4. What are their vocabulary patterns? (I.e., educated, precise, vulgar, etc.)

5. What is their demeanor when communicating? (I.e., cool and confident, nervous, etc.)

6. What posture do they tend to have?

7. Do they use gestures frequently in communication? If so, how often?

8. What are their common body language gestures or signals? (i.e., nail-biting, clenching fists, shoving hands in pockets, etc.)

Daily Behaviors & Habits

1. How does this character manage their finances? (i.e., saves a lot, living paycheck to paycheck, etc.)

2. Do they acquire any of their finances illegally? If so, how?

3. Do they have any personal habits that may be based on addictions? (i.e., drinking, smoking, gambling, etc.)

4. What is their morning routine? Be specific.

5. What does their average day look like? Be specific.

6. Do they ever have lunch in any particular spot?

7. What is your character's dinner routine? Be specific.

8. What does your character do after dinner? Be specific.

9. What is your character's bedtime routine? Be specific.

10. Does your character have any skills or talents? If so, do they share them or are they hidden and/or kept private?

11. What is your character unskilled at, or bad at? How do they feel about these flaws?

12. Do they have any hobbies?

Character's Past

1. Where is your character's hometown?

2. What was their childhood like? Do they remember it?

3. What is their earliest memory?

4. What is their saddest memory?

5. What is their happiest memory?

6. Did your character attend school? If so, how much? Did they enjoy school? Why or why not?

7. What is the most significant event that took place in your character's childhood?

8. Do they have any other significant childhood events?

9. What past jobs have they had that are significant to them?

10. Do they have a criminal record?

11. If your character does have a criminal record, how did they get it and where were they when the event happened?

12. Did they get any convictions or sentences? Did they serve time?

13. Who was the first person that your character loved?

14. When was their first sexual experience? Do think
    look back on it as a positive memory or a negative
    one?

15. Has your character experienced any major accidents
    or traumas in their life? If so, are they still affected
    by them? How?

Family Tree

1. Who is your character's mother? What is her full name?

2. Is she alive or deceased?

3. What is or was the mother's occupation?

4. What is the relationship that your character shares with their mother?

5. Who is your character's father? What is his full name?

6. Is he alive or deceased?

7. What is or was the father's occupation?

8. What is the relationship that your character shares with their father?

9. Does the character have any additional parental figures, such as a step-parent, foster parents, adoptive parents, biological parents, or even an adult who was of parental influence in their life such as a close family friend?

10. If they were adopted, do they know about it?

11. Does your character have any siblings? If so, list them by age in birth order. Include their names and how they are related to the character. (i.e., full sibling, step-sibling, half-sibling, etc.)

12. What type of relationship does your character share with each of their siblings?

13. Does your character have any nieces or nephews? If so, what are the relationship(s) like?

14. Do they have any in-laws? If so, what are the relationship(s) like?

15. Who else is a part of the character's family that is significant to the story, aside from those already listed?

Relationships

1. Who is your character's best or closest friend? How long have they known each other and where did they meet?

2. Do they have any other close friends? If so, how long has your character known them and where did they meet?

3. How is your character perceived by their friends?

4. How is your character perceived by strangers?

5. How is your character perceived by their spouse or lover?

6. How is your character perceived by their past spouses/lovers?

7. How is your character perceived by their children, if they have any?

8. How is your character perceived by their other family members?

9. How is your character perceived by the opposite
    sex?

10. How is your character perceived by children in
    general?

11. How is your character perceived by others who have
    more success than them?

12. How is your character perceived by others who have
    less success than them?

13. How is your character perceived by their boss, if
    they have one?

14. How is your character perceived by their co-
    workers?

15. How is your character perceived by their
    competitors?

16. How is your character perceived by authorities? (i.e.,
    police, doctors, attorneys, etc.)

17. How does your character react to people who
    challenge them?

18. How does your character react to people who anger them?

19. How does your character react to people who ask for help?

20. What do others tend to like most about your character?

21. What do they like least or consider to be the character's biggest flaw?

22. Does this character have any secret attractions to others? If so, have they been explored?

23. In romantic relationships, is your character typically faithful or unfaithful? If they are unfaithful, does their partner(s) know it?

24. What are they like during sexual encounters? (inhibited and shy or outgoing and wild?) Does this change over the course of the story or their life? If it does, why?

25. Who does your character like the least out of everyone in the story? Why?

26. Who does your character like the most out of everyone in the story? Why?

27. Who does your character consider to be the most important person in their life right now, and why do they feel this way?

28. Who is your character romantically attracted to at the moment, and why?

29. Who is your character's role model or idol? Why? And are they famous, or no?

30. Who does your character consider to be their enemy, if anyone?

31. Who does your character tend to misjudge or misunderstand the most?

32. Who tends to misunderstand or misjudge your character the most?

33. Is there anyone whom your character has lost touch within their lifetime who was significant to them? If so, why and how has it affected your character?

34. What was the worst ending to any relationship your character has had? (romantic or otherwise)

35. Who do they typically rely on when it comes to receiving advice?

36. Who does your character tend to rely on when it comes to emotional support?

37. Who does your character support, either emotionally or with advice, the most?

Attitude & Beliefs

1. Does your character have any psychological issues such as phobias, mental illnesses, or otherwise?

2. Do they tend to be optimistic or pessimistic?

3. Do you know the Meyer Briggs personality type for your character? (This can give a lot of information about how they would react and respond in a variety of situations.)

4. When is your character the most comfortable in life? (i.e., when drinking, when with certain people, when alone, etc.)

5. When are they the least comfortable? (i.e., when public speaking, in certain locations, around certain people, when drinking, etc.)

6. Does your character tend to be cautious, reckless, or brave in how they approach their life?

7. What does your character value and prioritize the most? (i.e., family, religion, friends, fun, money, success, etc.)

8. Who does your character love the best?

9. What or who would your character be willing to die for?

10. How does your character tend to be towards others? (i.e., compassionate, arrogant, selfish, sensitive, etc.)

11. What is the personal philosophy of your character?

12. What is your character most embarrassed about?

13. What is their greatest wish?

14. Do they have any prejudices against other people? If so, what and why?

15. What are their political beliefs?

16. Do they believe in any superstitions, fate, or destiny?

17. What is the greatest strength that your character possesses?

18. What is the greatest weakness that your character possesses?

19. What other positive or strong characteristics does your character possess?

20. What other negative or weak characteristics does your character possess?

21. What does your character favor most about their own attributes? (Both physical and personality-wise)

22. What does your character despise most about their own attributes? (Both physical and personality-wise)

23. Are these feelings accurate, or are they over or underplayed?

24. How does your character think other people perceive them? Is this accurate?

25. What does your character regret the most in life?

26. Do they have any other regrets?

27. What are the biggest secrets that your character has?

28. Does anyone else know about these secrets? If so, who?

29. How do they react in a crisis?

30. What tends to cause the most problems in their life? (i.e., finances, colleagues, friends, family, health, etc.)

31. How do they react to change?

32. Do they have any quirks?

33. What would your character like to change about themselves the most?

34. Give a short paragraph (100 words or less) of the character describing themselves to others.

35. What are their short-term goals?

36. What are their long-term goals?

37. Do they have any plans to achieve the goals, or do they believe they are out of reach?

38. How would others be affected by your character reaching these goals? Do this effects matter to your character?

39. If anything is stopping your character from achieving their goals, what is it?

40. What are they actively working to protect, keep, or gain right now?

41. What event or situation do they most fear or dread being in?

42. What person would your character want to be, if they could be anyone?

43. Who would they absolutely not want to be?

Likes & Favorites

1. What is your character's favorite food?

2. What is your character's favorite drink?

3. What color do they like most?

4. Do they have a favorite book?

5. Do they have a favorite film?

6. What song or music genre do they prefer?

7. Do they watch TV? If so, what do they watch?

8. Does your character have a favorite sport?

9. Does your character have a motto or a quote that they like?

10. Where do they like to hang out or spend most of their time?

11. What do they own that is their favorite possession?

This list may seem extremely exhausting, but trust that all of this information will help you get to know your character intimately. Once you have the answers to all of these questions, you will know your character so well that it will be effortless for you to write about them and their natural evolution over the course of your novel. Do your best to fill in the entire questionnaire so that you have plenty of material to write on and that nothing is left up to chance. A writer who has extremely strong characters is one who knows their characters so well that they could easily answer any of these questions about them. Keep your character profile handy so that you can refer back to it during the writing process as needed.

A Word on Minor Characters

Naturally, you don't need to have an elaborate profile for your minor characters. Instead, go through the list and pick the questions that you feel relate most to how the character fits into the story. For example, if it is a friend from high school that your protagonist sees once or twice during the entire book, you likely don't need to include much. You may want to fill out the general section, the past section, and the likes and favorites section. Even then, it may not be necessary for you to fill out the entire thing. When it comes to designing minor characters, use your judgment to create a character that has depth, without wasting your time developing a character further than you actually need to for the benefit of your overall book.

Chapter 4: Creating Expression

How your character expresses themselves is a really important part of how they contribute to the story itself. Their expression is ultimately how your character conveys themselves to others. This will be how they express their thoughts and opinions, and how they portray themselves to others to interpret them and who they are. You want to make sure that, just like with your character development, you develop how your character expresses themselves as well. While this part of the book will not go into as elaborate of a guide as the previous chapter did, we will explore various ways that you can create an expression for your character, as well as for all of the characters within' your book as a whole.

Catch Phrases

Having characters have their own catchphrases is a great way to build an expression in your character and give them a unique voice. This should be a catchphrase that only one character uses, even though other characters may sometimes paraphrase that character to be funny or to otherwise quote them. Still, it should be known that this phrase is unique to that specific character.

Don't overuse catch phrases in your book or it will take away from the value of them. Ideally, only one or *maybe* two characters should have a catch phrase in your book. Also, avoid it being the main character unless they are only going to use the catchphrase from time to time. The catch phrase is a great way to give foreshadowing effects, but with too many, it can take away and just sound cheesy or poorly written.

Group-Specific Slang Words

If you look at most friend groups in real life, they have their own way of speaking. This way of speaking often includes their own selection of slang words. If you want to increase the expression and voice of your overall group, as well as each character that is a part of it, seek to make slang words or group mottos that are used by everyone in the group. However, make sure that none of the slang or mottos are anywhere close to the one character's catchphrase or you will confuse the reader. Instead, simply choose expressions and terms that this group will speak in that others likely don't. This makes them unique and gives them a very realistic feel, since this is completely natural behavior in real life, too.

Other Worldly Slang

If you are writing a fantasy book that takes your characters to another world, consider using other worldly slang that you have made up in order to help set them apart. In a group, each person speaks differently from one another, just as how each individual in a country – or likely the entire world – speaks differently. You likely wouldn't go to a different planet and hear everyone speaking in typical American dialect. For that reason, it is a good idea to create and include other worldly phrases and slang that help the reader differentiate the characters.

Gender-Specific Phrases

If you ever pay attention to a real-life crowd, men and women tend to express themselves in extremely different ways. You can bring this type of gender-specific expression into your novel, too. And, in fact, you should. By including as many different unique elements of expression in your novel as you can, you make the novel more believable, and your readers have an easier time relating to it. While you don't have to use gender stereotypes to create the expressions between each gender, you should make it clear that they are two different genders speaking and expressing themselves. If you need inspiration, spend some time with a group of males and then spend some time with a group of females and you will see the differences. If you want to take it even further, afterward spend some time with a mixed group and you will still notice that each gender expresses themselves differently, even in front of the other sex.

Career and Industry Jargon

People in different careers and industries typically speak in unique tongues. They have industry and career-specific jargon that they use when they are talking to their colleagues. When you are building characters who have jobs, careers, or are heavily involved in certain industries, make sure that you include some jargon from that job, career, or industry in their vocabulary. In the real world, people would naturally pick up on and use this jargon. Therefore, your character should too.

Body Language

It is no secret that body language is a major part of how we communicate with others and express ourselves. Use body language in your book, too. If characters are feeling attacked or bullied and they are feeling particularly low or closed off, have them standing with a closed expression such as with their arms crossed and skulking away from the attacker. If the character is happy, have them standing tall and proud with their body casual but a bright smile on their face. Using body language as a means to help your characters communicate on an even more advanced level will help you when it comes to expressing your characters. While you don't need to explain their body language at every moment, a good idea is to introduce what they look like when they're feeling neutral and then only talk about their body language if it is vastly different from what it would be when they're in that neutral state. If you are unsure about what body language people would be using when they're talking or when they're feeling different things, consider briefly studying it. There are many online and print resources available that are made specifically to help people further understand body language. Knowing it more intimately may help you when it comes to helping your character express themselves.

Sometimes when you are creating certain scenes, body language can speak more to the reader and other characters than the communicating character's own words will. For example, if the character is lying to someone else, have their words telling a lie while their body exposes the truth about them lying. Maybe they are telling a lie, and in the meantime, they are sweating, and they have shoved their hands into their pockets. Body language can teach people a lot about what is truly going on in your character's mind, beyond what they say, so be sure to use it at the appropriate times for greater expression.

Dialect

Make sure your character's dialect is true to where they come from. If they are from the southern states, for example, have them use a southern dialect. You may even have presented their accent to the reader. If they are from somewhere else, such as a foreign country, use the dialect that is natural to where that person comes from. Using proper native dialect not only helps create a realistic element to your characters but it also helps you contrast between your characters if you have a few that are from different areas or countries.

Regional Slang

Most regions have their own slang that is unique from other regions. Just like their dialect differs from place to place, so too does their choice in slang words. In the majority of cases kids and teens are more likely to use slang over adults, so make sure that the younger demographic uses a lot more slang than the older demographic. Furthermore, ensure that the slang that your younger demographic is using is age specific and that your older demographic is using age-specific terms. The adults may occasionally use terms from the younger demographic, but don't make this happen often and make sure that you make it clear that they have borrowed it from someone in the younger generation.

General Vocabulary

In addition to all of the other steps in this chapter, make sure that you take a look at your character's vocabulary in general. Everyone tends to speak a certain way, often slightly different from other people. To put it bluntly, there are some people that just don't say some things because it's not a part of their standard vocabulary. The best thing to do is to get an idea of what your character's overall vocabulary is. Since vocabulary and the words, they could use go so far, the better idea is to outline what they don't say and would never say. This helps you get an idea for their style of communication and what they actually would say.

Creating expression takes time and practice, but if you follow these tips and have patience, you should be well on your way to creating strong terms of expression for all of your characters. Remember, when it comes to really planning out each character, don't worry too much about creating a very specific set of expressions for characters who have an extremely minor role in the story. Instead, focus on those who are minor but recurring, or those who are central characters. These are the ones who you really want to go into depth with when planning their expressions. Take your time and work through each of these steps while planning out how the character will express themselves in each one and use this as your opportunity to get to know your character even more. This will make it much simpler to know how your character will express themselves and communicate with others in your novel.

Chapter 5: Bringing Your Character to Life

Finally, you want to bring your character to life! This is the part of the process where you take that perfect profile you've made on paper, and you start bringing each character to life for the first time. This is where you get to turn them into real characters that will have prominent roles in your novel in one way or another. Through the following steps, you will tie up any loose ends and then ultimately unleash your character into the world. Once this part of the process is done, you can start writing your story, trusting that your characters will be strong enough to support the plot line and make your story truly great.

Use Inspiration from People You Actually Know

There is a good chance that the characters you have made somehow resemble someone you already know in real life. When we are creating characters, we are often drawn on inspiration from those that we already know. Don't feel shy when doing this! When you are writing, feel open to the idea of drawing on more inspiration for situations where you might need it. For example, if you are truly struggling to identify how your character would act, react, respond, or speak in any given situation, draw inspiration from that person! This will help their actions flow naturally so that they seem realistic to who the character truly is. It is never a bad thing to draw on this inspiration, so keep it handy and use it at your own discretion to help increase the quality of your story, simplify the writing process, and create a compelling character that fits perfectly into your story.

Play on the Element of Surprise

Sometimes readers expect a certain thing when they are reading. For example, if your characters are going into a night club your reader will likely expect that the bouncer is some big gangly guy who would easily knock anyone down who tried to slip through uninvited. Instead of simply going with the person that your reader would assume the character would look like, pick someone unique who makes your reader feel surprised towards who is playing the role. For example, you might pick a slender and somewhat lanky character who looks like they would struggle to keep a small dog back, let alone a potential customer who was serious about getting in. Instead of having a tall, white, male lawyer, consider having someone from a completely different demographic. Character's don't need to be exactly who you would assume they would be. In fact, they're often better when they aren't whom you expect them to be, yet this is still phenomenal at their role.

In addition to using the element of surprise in your characters, use it in your events, too. Don't be afraid to make the unexpected happen and keep your readers on their toes. Use events that they wouldn't have expected create settings that are unlike what they would have expected, and ultimately give your reader a reason to think "Oh, wow! Really?" This element of surprise is a great way to bring your characters and book itself to life. Most real-life experiences don't go as planned and often many unexpected events, people, and circumstances come to light in our lives. Do the same with your book, both with characters, events, and circumstances. You want your reader to feel like it is real life and that they never know what to expect from one day to another. This increases the value of your story and also heightens your reader's engagement and commitment towards your book.

Use Contradictions

Strong characters often have qualities that are highly contradictory. People aren't always as they seem, and so your character's shouldn't be as well. A great way to increase the livelihood of your characters and bring them to life is to give them contradictions. For example, an incredibly sporty race car driver who is obsessed with the opera. Using these contradictions in your characters remind people that they're human and that they aren't always logical box-fitting characters. Instead, they are real, and they have interesting quirks about them just like we all do.

Give Your Characters Goals

In the character developing chapter we explored the goals that your character has, but now we really want to emphasize on that. Giving your character's goals, hopes, dreams, and fantasies about how they want the future to be for themselves make them a lot more life-like. Real life people always have some form of goal or dream, whether they talk about it or not. Giving your characters these features is important because it gives them something to look forward to, and something for your reader to look forward to with them. It gives your reader a deeper insight into your character's inner world and what makes them tick, therefore making your reader feel a lot more connected to your character.

Discover Their Image

Through the character development process, we discovered many identifying factors that shed light on what your character's actual image was, but if you really want to make them life-like, you want to discover exactly what it is like. One great way to do this is to find a picture of someone on Google or otherwise who represents your character. They should look similar both in physical appearances and in the way they present themselves through style and expression. Many great writers claim that they will even print these pictures off and keep them nearby so that they can truly look at their characters and gain insight from them during the writing process, to help progress the story along. If this feels right for you, certainly go ahead and borrow this tip from other writers.

One thing to note about your character's image is that despite you know it intimately, you don't want to over explain it to your readers. Instead, give away important pieces of information but let your reader develop a picture in their own mind. When your reader generates their own image of who your character is and what they look like it becomes more engaging and more personal. Then, your reader is more likely to connect with your character and feel a form of emotional attachment towards them.

Listen to Them

Many writers claim that they can actually *hear* their character's voices. They start often by hearing a voice on the television or somewhere in public that sounds extremely similar to their character's own voice. Then, they listen to that person and try to generate a total voice from it. Through that, they are able to listen to the voice of the character and use that to help them move forward.

Each character has their own unique voice. This is a combination of how they speak, what they are saying, and all of the tone and emotion that goes into their words. You want to discover the voice of each of your characters when you are writing because this makes the sense of expression and speaking for them much easier. This is where you get the opportunity to bring them to life because they become a voice that, eventually, everybody hears somewhere. They may also hear it through someone on television or in public, but ultimately they can relate it back and go "hey that sounds like so and so from that book I just read!" When this happens, you have truly made your character life-like to the highest degree.

Practice

It may take some time, but as with all things, you need to practice. Practicing bringing your characters to life and making them realistic is a great way to truly discover how you can do it to the highest of your abilities. At first, it may feel uncomfortable or even unnatural, but quickly you will find an opportunity to make your characters even more life-like, and it will all just flow together.

One great way to practice is to consider an everyday situation. It doesn't have to be one that is going to be involved in your book, just consider an everyday situation, such as going into a coffee shop and talking to the barista. Then, write a few paragraphs for each character that you are trying to bring to life. Consider how they would walk into the café, how they would communicate with the barista, where they would go to stand after they've ordered, how they would carry their coffees, whether they would drink the coffee there or go elsewhere. Consider whether they have someone with them or if they're alone. How do they express themselves to other patrons in the coffee shop? Get very specific about how their visit would go through these paragraphs. This is a great way to really consider how your character would react in everyday situations, thus making it a lot easier for you to get to know your own character personally. Remember, once you know them intimately it becomes a lot easier to share them with your readers.

Give Your Characters Plenty of Opportunities to Show Up

Giving your character the opportunity to show the reader how they react in different situations is a great way to bring them to life. Put your characters into many different situations and give your reader the opportunity to see them in action in every single one. Share about how your character acts in these situations, what they are thinking, and what they say. Let your reader have an idea of what your character's intentions are and perhaps even what got them into this situation in the first place.

Giving your character plenty of chances to show up and experience many different situations that they can take action in gives you the opportunity to highlight them from different angles. You can show your reader what that character is like when they're angry, sad, happy, disappointed, unimpressed, hurt, and virtually any other emotion. When you explore your character under these different lights through naturally unfolding events, you make it a lot easier for you to give your reader a more intimate view of your character, too.

Successful stories are those that bring characters to life and make readers believe that they are real people. If you think back to any fiction novel you have read in the past, you can likely conclude that the best ones were the ones where you grieved the end of the book because it felt like you had truly lost someone from your life. *That's* how good your characters can become when you follow these guides and effectively bring them to life for your readers. And, although it may seem difficult, it truly isn't. Follow these steps, and you will have a life-like character playing on the heartstrings of your own readers in no time.

Conclusion

Thank you for reading *"Character Development: Step-by-Step | Essential Story Character Creation, Character Expression and Character Building Tricks Any Writer Can Learn"*.

I hope that you were able to learn plenty of information about how you can create a phenomenal character for your own novel throughout this book. By using the in-depth character creation guide, following the tips on how to build your character, how to make them great, and how to bring them to life, you should have all of the tools you need to make a phenomenal character that will truly draw your readers in and help them generate a sense of emotional attachment to your characters.

The next step is to begin building your characters. If you haven't already, take the time to generate a profile for each of your central characters and all of your biggest minor characters. As well, create modified profiles for your minor characters. Remember that they don't need to be nearly as in-depth, but they do still need to be descriptive enough that you can create a truly strong character. Furthermore, make sure that you pay attention to the tips about how you can make a good character great, and about how you can then bring your characters to life. Ideally, your characters should be brought to life and made so great that your readers feel as though they are friends with that character. They may even grieve the loss of the character when the book ends, and there is nothing left for them to read. Using these tools and tricks, you can certainly create characters that good for your own novel.

Thank you, and best of luck! Have fun writing!